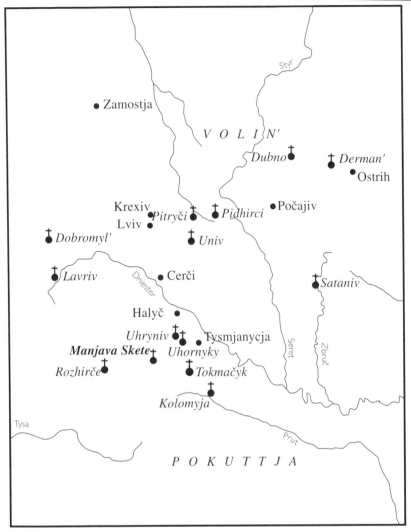

Zamostja

V O L I N'

Dubno ✝ *Derman'*
Ostrih

Krexiv
Pitryči ✝ *Pidhirci* *Počajiv*
Lviv
✝ *Dobromyl'* *Univ*

✝ *Lavriv* *Cerči* ✝ *Sataniv*

Dniester

Halyč

Uhryniv ✝ *Tysmjanycja*
Manjava Skete ✝ *Uhornyky*
Rozhirče ✝ *Tokmačyk*

Kolomyja

Tysa

Seret

Zbruč

Prut

P O K U T T J A

Styr

Eastern Europe in the Early Seventeenth Century, detail.

CISTERCIAN STUDIES SERIES: NUMBER ONE HUNDRED NINETY-TWO

SOPHIA SENYK

MANJAVA SKETE

UKRAINIAN MONASTIC WRITINGS
OF THE SEVENTEENTH CENTURY

CISTERCIAN STUDIES SERIES: NUMBER ONE HUNDRED NINETY-TWO

MANJAVA SKETE

Ukrainian Monastic Writings of the Seventeenth Century

Translated, with an Introduction,

by

Sophia Senyk

Cistercian Publications
Kalamazoo–Spencer–Coalville

ISBN 0 87907 592 9

Cistercian Publications

BX
729.5
.A4
M36
2001

Editorial Offices and Customer Service
Institute of Cistercian Studies
Western Michigan University
1903 W. Michigan Avenue
Kalamazoo, MI 49008–5415
cistpub@wmich.edu

Warehouse
Saint Joseph's Abbey
Spencer, MA 01562

UK Customer Service
97 Loughborough Road
Thringstone, Coalville, Leics. LE67 8LQ
MsbcistP@aol.com
www.spencerabbey.org/cistpub

The work of Cistercian Publications
is made possible in part by support from Western Michigan University
to The Institute of Cistercian Studies

The editors express their appreciation to
the following persons for their assistance:
Robert De Lossa and The Ukrainian
Research Institute of Harvard University
Stefan Sarenius, Maps Coordinator of the
University Libraries, Western Michigan University
Meghan Russell, Editorial Assistant, Cistercian Publications
Paola Pastore, Graphic Designer, Cistercian Publications

TABLE OF CONTENTS

LIST OF WORKS CITED
IN ABBREVIATED FORM

AJuZR   *Архив юго-западной России [Arxiv*
               jugozapadnoj Rossii]. Part I. 12 volumes. Kiev,
               1859–1914
Baguenard   *Dans la tradition basilienne.* Spiritualité
               orientale 58. Abbaye de Bellefontaine, 1994
Basil, *reg.*   *Asceticon parvum*
Basil, *reg.fus.* *Regulae fusius tractatae*
Celevyč   Юліян Целевич. *Исторія Скиту*
               Манявского. [Julijan Celevyč. *Istorija Skytu*
               Manjavskoho]. Lviv 1887
Clarke   *The Ascetic Works of Saint Basil.* Translated
               W. K. L. Clarke. London: Society for
               Promoting Christian Knowledge, 1925
Climacus   John Climacus. *The Ladder of Divine Ascent.*
               Page numbers refer to the translation by
               Colm Luibhead and Norman Russell. The
               Classics of Western Spirituality series. New
               York: Paulist Press, 1982
CS   Cistercian Studies series. Spencer,
               Washington D.C., Kalamazoo, 1969–
Featherstone   *The Life of Paisij Velyčkovs'kyj.* Tr. J. M. E.
               Featherstone. HLEUL 4. Cambridge MA:
               Ukrainian Research Institute of Harvard
               University, 1989
HLEUL   Harvard Library of Early Ukrainian
               Literature. English Translations. Cambridge
               MA: Ukrainian Research Institute of
               Harvard University, 1989–.
NPNF   A Select Library of Nicene and Post-Nicene
               Fathers of the Christian Church. Second

Series. 14 volumes. Reprint. Grand Rapids: Wm. B. Eerdmans Publishing Company, 1978 (and other reprinting dates)

PG   J.-P. Migne. Patrologiae cursus completus, series graeca, 162 volumes. Paris, 1857–1866.

Russell   *The Lives of the Desert Fathers. The* Historia Monachorum *in Aegypto.* Translated Norman Russell. CS 34. Kalamazoo: Cistercian Publications, 1981

Wagner   *Saint Basil. Ascetical Works.* Translated Monica Wagner. The Fathers of the Church. A New Translation 9. Washington D.C.: The Catholic University of America Press 1950

Wheeler   *Dorotheos of Gaza. Discourses and Sayings.* Translated Eric P. Wheeler osb. CS 33. Kalamazoo: Cistercian Publications, 1977

INTRODUCTION

IN THE UKRAINIAN CARPATHIAN Mountains, in a remote spot an enclosure with a tower and some modern reconstruction of buildings typical of that region draws numerous persons, both tourists and pilgrims. They come to visit what remains of a monastery that was suppressed two centuries ago, in an age that professed an enlightened belief in a Supreme Being, but found the silent praise of that Being superfluous. The pilgrims who for two hundred years have continued to visit that spot testify to the spiritual force of the monastery that stood there from about 1605 until 1785, the Manjava Skete.

The term skete, in Ukrainian *skyt*, designates small monasteries in remote localities. Properly speaking, a skete is a very small monastic community with a handful of members, always distant from inhabited centers. A skete exists in solitude, *pustynja*, which literally means desert. Solitude, and the silence that accompanies it, encourage a similar quieting of the human soul so that it can be attentive to God; they favor *hesychia*, stillness, the condition for a continuous remembrance of God, uninterrupted prayer.

Manjava, like other influential sketes, could not remain small, but it preserved its primitive spirit throughout its existence. It also preserved its primitive way of life in a little skete, a *skytyk*, where the solitary cell of its founder had stood.

The way of life of the monastic community at Manjava and the spirit instilled by its founder is described in the works translated in this volume:

—the *Life* of the founder of Manjava Skete, Jov
    Knjahynyc'kyj;

9

—the *Testament* of Theodosius, whom Jov placed as
superior of the Skete;
—and the *Rule* for the *skytyk*, in which Theodosius set
down what was in fact already the practice.

All three works were written around the middle of the
seventeenth century. They not only give evidence of Manjava's founding and early years by persons who were either
witnesses or very close to the origins, but testify to the continuation of the original inspiration that marked monastic
life at Manjava.

The period in which Jov settled in a solitary cell at
Manjava saw many anachoretic settlements in Ukraine.
A good number of them, like Manjava, developed into
cenobitic monasteries and their origins as solitary cells or
small sketes usually went unrecorded, to be lost forever or
to be buried in hagiographic or monastic legend.

Fortunately for posterity, one of the the early monks
of Manjava Skete, Ignatius, had the gifts of a first-rate
biographer. We know nothing about him except what he
says in the *Life* itself and in its codicil. He was by origin
from the small town Ljubariv and joined Jov's community
still at Uhornyky, then followed Jov to Manjava. Thus he was
a companion and eyewitness of almost all of Jov's monastic
life in Ukraine.

Ignatius was steeped in traditional monastic writings,
including hagiography; his language echoes this literature,
as it does that of the Office and Scripture. But he possessed
a skilled pen, he was not bound by the conventions of
hagiography and he had the good sense to let facts speak
for themselves. He saw the founder of Manjava Skete as one
in a long succession of monastic fathers, but his customary
reading and his veneration for Jov did not mislead him—
as they have misled others in similar circumstances—to
present Jov' life as a repetition of edifying incidents culled
from the lives of assorted holy fathers. Precise references to
persons and places and exact dates inspire confidence, as

does also the absence of astounding wonders. Ignatius does not embellish his account with marvels worked by Jov in the hope of edifying his readers and eliciting their admiration, but soberly he describes the long and toil-filled life of a monk whose one aim was to live wholly in God. This very sobriety is nowhere more effective than in the detailed description of Jov's death. The restraint of Ignatius is more moving than any effusiveness and gives us a clear picture of what Jov meant for the monks who were his direct disciples.

One able author is already an exception in monasteries of that time and place, especially a monastery to which literary pursuits were foreign, but Manjava was blessed with a second writer, Theodosius. Jov's *Life* recounts how Theodosius arrived soon after Jov settled at Manjava, how Jov sent him to another monastery to gain experience in living in a community, knowing that the young hierodeacon would return when the time was ripe, how Theodosius indeed returned as soon as he heard that the condition imposed by Jov was about to be fulfilled, and how Jov made him the superior and the spiritual father of the Manjava monks. The intimate collaboration of Theodosius with Jov, his sharing of Jov's ideals, brought him the honor of being called, in the codicil of the copy of his *Testament*, a founder of the Manjava Skete.

Theodosius put the *Rule* for the *skytyk* in writing, thus fixing the primitive observance of Manjava which the *skytyk* was to maintain. In addition, he was moved in his old age to write his spiritual *Testament*, which mirrors the customs and spirit of his monastery.

In the three works presented here we have, then, a *Life* of the founder, Jov Knjahynyc'kyj; an account of the founding and early years of Manjava Skete; a *Rule* that reflects how Jov lived with the first disciples who gathered around him and how their way of life was maintained even after a large community was formed; and the instructions of the superior Theodosius, which show how the Skete community continued in the spirit of its founder about half a century after its beginnings.

To appreciate the import of Manjava Skete and of the writings presented in this volume, we must see them in the context of ukrainian and, more broadly, Eastern monasticism, especially of the hesychast current of monastic spirituality that Manjava typifies.

Monasticism in Ukraine

Monastic life in what is present-day Ukraine began to be recorded about half a century after the baptism of Kievan Rus' in 988. We can leave aside the presence of foreign, primarily greek monks, who accompanied greek hierarchs to Rus', and a few monastic foundations by princes, about which we have no particulars and which were small in size and perhaps also peopled at first by greek monks. The history of monasticism in Ukraine begins properly with Saint Antony of the Caves († about 1073). We are poorly informed about Antony's life, since his early *vita* has not survived and, in any case, appears to have leaned heavily towards hagiographical *topoi*. What is well-nigh certain is that Antony started out as a monk on Mount Athos; he returned to his native land and settled in a cave near Kiev around 1051. Soon disciples began to arrive, wanting to live with him. As their number grew, Antony appointed a superior and blessed the founding of a monastery with cells and a church above ground, while he himself continued to lead a solitary life in his cave. The organization of the monastery proper at the Kiev Caves owes most to an early disciple of Antony, Theodosius (†1074). Saints Antony and Theodosius of the Caves are rightfully regarded as the co-founders and patrons of all monasticism in Rus', hence in what is today Ukraine, Belarus, and Russia.[1]

---

1. For a fuller treatment, with the background history of Christianity in Rus', see S. Senyk, *A History of the Church in Ukraine*, Vol. I: To the End of the

From Jov's life it will be seen that the monastic experience of Antony is strikingly repeated at the origins of the Manjava Skete: a monk of decided eremitical bent, professed on Mount Athos, sets out to live as an anchorite, but becomes in spite of himself the founder of a monastic cenobium. He then turns over its government to another and himself continues to pursue the solitary life, insofar as the importunities of others allow him. This pattern is repeated not only at the Manjava Skete, but at the beginnings of many other monasteries in Ukraine. The similarities between the Kiev Caves monastery and Manjava Skete is not a matter of external coincidences, but reflects ideals in ukrainian monasticism that derive from Antony's foundation and that were never extinguished, as we shall see from examples below.

From the Mongol invasion of 1240 until the early seventeenth century, present-day Ukraine east of the Dnieper river—a plain with no natural barriers for protection—was prey to continuous raids from the East and also from the South, especially after the formation of the Tatar khanate in the Crimea in the fifteenth century. The eastern half of present-day Ukraine therefore was sparsely settled, and even that only in its northern reaches, so there was little monastic life in those parts. Monasticism in Ukraine, until the seventeenth century, was concentrated west of the Dnieper. In the course of the seventeenth and eighteenth centuries, however, numerous monasteries and sketes arose also in Ukraine east of the Dnieper River.

When we try to create a list or a statistical table of these monasteries, we begin to grasp one distinctive aspect of

---

Thirteenth Century, Orientalia Christiana Analecta 243 (Rome: Pontificio Istituto Orientale, 1993). The origins of the Kiev Caves Monastery, the life of Theodosius, and anecdotes about its early monks are recounted in *The Paterik of the Kievan Caves Monastery,* translated Muriel Heppell, HLEUL, 1 (Cambridge, MA: Ukrainian Research Institute of Harvard University, 1989). The *Life* of Theodosius is also included in *The Hagiography of Kievan Rus',* translated Paul Hollingsworth, HLEUL, 2 (Cambridge, MA: Ukrainian Research Institute of Harvard University, 1992).

this monasticism. Monasteries in or close to towns were stable institutions; we can often determine the date of the foundation to within the decade. The further one follows ukrainian monasteries into woods, desolate river banks, and inaccessible mountain slopes, the less definable they become. Lavriv, founded in the Carpathian Mountains as a settlement of anchorites living in scattered cells in the thirteenth century; Počajiv, founded at the end of the sixteenth century around a solitary cell, on a ridge overlooking a vast plain in Volyn'; Krexiv, founded around a solitary cell on a wooded hillside in the early seventeenth century—these and similar monasteries grew into large and permanent communities, but not all anchorite cells developed into monasteries. Many hermitages and sketes lasted only one or two generations; they may be mentioned in a descriptive source or they may have left a trace in a place name—as the many examples of Monastyr, Monastyrok, Čerči (from a word meaning monk), and similar terms in ukrainian toponomy testify—but no further record remains of their existence.

Anachoretism was also known in the West, but long before the seventeenth century it had all but disappeared from the latin Church. Where it existed, as among the Carthusians and the Camaldolese, it was wholly institutionalized. The western development of monastic orders, with well-defined rules and organization, coupled with ecclesiastical legislation that frowned on solitaries outside the monastic orders, led to the disappearance of this form of monastic life.

The high esteem in which anachoretism continued to be held in the lands of eastern Christianity, on the other hand, supported a striving for the solitary life, chosen out of a deeply felt spiritual need, and often the anchorites' way of life attracted disciples. The current of solitary monasticism was especially strong in Ukraine; it flourished well into the eighteenth century, when increasing pressure from the state led to its disappearance.

Another feature of ukrainian monasticism, which is first seen in the life of Saint Antony of the Caves, is its ties with Mount Athos. Antony of the Caves had come to Kiev after beginning his monastic life on Mount Athos and he came with the blessing of the Holy Mountain. The monastic settlement on Athos, especially after the founding of the Great Lavra by Saint Athanasius of Athos in 963, has been the ideal monastic milieu of the byzantine tradition. Athos is often idealized, but whatever the actual quality of monastic life there—and admittedly the average level was often not very high—it served as a beacon. Those who truly sought God alone could always find the conditions for their quest on the Holy Mountain. For this we have testimony from all periods, and one of these is the early *podvyh* of Jov *Knjahynyc'kyj*. Monastic observance on Athos was not at its greatest flourishing at the end of the sixteenth century, but providentially Jov came upon an elder who initiated him into an authentic spiritual life and who then directed him to Vatopedi just as that monastery was undergoing a reform—short-lived, to be sure—that restored common life.

The link with Athos and the solitary life, from the times of Saint Antony of the Caves and ever after, were viewed in Ukraine as the marks of genuine monastic life. This did not come from legends which created imaginary solitaries returning from Athos to become founders of monasteries; numerous authentic sources show that many monasteries did grow up around the cells of solitaries, many of whom had indeed spent some time on Athos. Many other such cells attracted disciples during the lifetime of the solitary, but did not develop into monasteries.

Every important monastery in Ukraine traced its beginnings to the cell of a solitary. When written documents were lacking, pious tradition took their place, a tradition that seldom needed to be invented. From Hustyn' in the eastern reaches to Dobromyl' in the mountainous western regions, the story is the same: two or three hermits, a tiny church, and then a monastic brotherhood following a common life. The mention of common life is another constant, and we shall return to it below. Hustyn' and Dobromyl' date from the end of the sixteenth or the beginning of the seventeenth century, as do the Počajiv and Krexiv monasteries mentioned above. We begin to glimpse the great ferment in monastic life in Ukraine in the period contemporary to the founding of Manjava Skete.[2]

The Times of Jov Knjahynyc'kyj

When Jov found the spot on which to settle and where the Manjava Skete would rise, he prayed:

> I beg you, my Master and Creator, raise again among our people the evangelical christian life that has waned, a monasticism lived with *podvyh* and common life according to your command-ments, for the renewal and adornment of your holy Church, as it was formerly in Rus', at the time of our holy fathers Antony and Theodosius and the others who shone forth in the cave in the town of Kiev. With the passing of time and a change of persons, piety has waned and the good order of monastic common life has been extinguished, and monasteries have become deserted.[3]

In fact, someone looking at monasticism in Ukraine in the sixteenth century could be pardoned for being skeptical about any possibility of its speedy revival. Monastic life shared the crisis of all church life, a crisis which was

2. For further details and these and related points, see S. Senyk, 'L'hésychasme dans le monachisme ukrainien', *Irénikon* (1989) 172–212.

3. *Life*, sec. 6.

not confined to ruthenian lands—present-day Ukraine and Belarus, which formed a single church province, at the head of which was the metropolitan of Kiev.

The humanism of the Renaissance had imposed on the Church in the West a worldly façade from which it began to recover only after it had been rent by the Protestant Reformation. The Church in ruthenian lands, like the Eastern Church in general, was not directly affected by this secular renaissance mentality. Yet it suffered from its consequences.

All ruthenian lands at that time were included in the Polish-Lithuanian state, and the policy by which the king and the magnates made appointments to high church posts, including to the post of superior of major monasteries— as they had the right to do—was based on cupidity, not concern for the Church's welfare. The posts often went to the highest bidder, who then used the church benefice for his own enrichment.

If to some extent the Ruthenian Church in the sixteenth century, and monasticism in particular, bear the marks of the ravages of western worldliness, they also share in the general climate of decline besetting the Church in the East. The dominance of the Muslim Ottomans over large portions of the Churches of the constantinopolitan tradition cannot be used as a handy scapegoat by which to excuse all the shortcomings of church life, but it was indeed to blame for many ills and offered little hope for a religious revival among eastern Christians. The Ruthenian Church belonged to the patriarchate of Constantinople, and although its internal development was not bound to the Constantinopolitan Church, it shared to some extent in its malaise. The immediate neighbors to the southwest were the romanian principalities of Wallachia and Moldavia, under the protectorate of the Ottoman Porte. These principalities, especially Moldavia, had many close cultural and religious ties with Rus'—that is, Ukraine; in that period their liturgical language was still Church Slavonic, as it was in Rus'; and Ruthenian, not Romanian, was used in official documents and religious literature. The *Life* of Jov shows the frequent contacts with moldavian monasteries—Manjava was not far from the border with Moldavia—and his disciple Theodosius began his monastic life in a moldavian monastery, Putna. But little Moldavia, beset with frequent political coups, could not assist in a religious revival.

To the north was Muscovy, with a strong Church supported by the state, but Muscovy, where the excesses of the reign of Ivan IV the Terrible were followed by several decades of internal disorders and foreign intervention, was in the eyes of ruthenian churchmen a barbarous and unattractive country.

The renewal of church life in ruthenian lands came from within; the will for reform sprang up in various classes of ruthenian society. The hierarchy sought to improve church life, among other means, through the union of their Church with Rome. Burghers and nobles banded together in church brotherhoods that promoted the pious practices of their members and supported churches, schools, almshouses, and monasteries. And there appeared monks, like Jov of Manjava, who through their lives brought about a monastic revival.

There had always been anchorites, but now they attracted others to the monastic life and so exerted a reforming influence on existing monasteries. The details of Jov's early life testify to a growing resurgence of church life in Ukraine.

As a boy Jov, baptized Ivan, attended a monastic school, a witness that monasticism had an interest in promoting church culture. The schooling boys like Jov received there was entirely religious. Once the elements of reading had been mastered, the pupils were set to learning the psalter. At the Univ monastery school his further instruction was likely confined to reading texts of the Church Fathers: John Chrysostom, Basil, Ephrem, Isaac, Dorotheus.

The school which Jov then attended in Ostrih had very recently been founded by Prince Basil (also known as Constantine) Ostroz'kyj. This wealthiest of ruthenian magnates acted out of a sense of duty in doing something to further the cultural elevation of his Church. Unfortunately, this, like many of the prince's enthusiasms, did not last long, but for a few decades the school turned out students with a sound basic education, in which the study of languages played an important part. The Balaban family, which later contributed greatly to Jov's foundation at Uhornyky, was also involved in the cultural revival of their Church. Like Ostroz'kyj at Ostrih, Bishop Gedeon Balaban at his family property in Strjatyn' founded a press, primarily for the printing of liturgical books.

The monk Ioan Vyšens'kyj, who visited his friend Jov when the latter was already a monk at Uhornyky, stands somewhat apart. His works, written with verve in a lively language one might not expect from an athonite ascetic, are an important landmark in ukrainian literature, but their contents were of too fundamentalist a stamp even for his contemporaries and co-religionists. They were read, but influenced no one and were printed only three hundred fifty years after his death. Along with his rejection of the Union with Rome, he rejected what he considered the contamination of western leaning and strove against the times to restrict culture to pious books of prayer. Jov of Manjava himself was engaged briefly in anti-uniate polemic, when, after the death of Gedeon Balaban, non-uniates feared that the Lviv see might go to a uniate bishop. This formed, however, only a brief episode in Jov's life, spent for the most part not only far from what might be called public concerns or 'the world', but in a cultivation of solitude.

THE FOUNDING OF MANJAVA

Jov became a monk on Mount Athos, but once fully imbued with the monastic spirit, he settled in his homeland, becoming a monastic founder. His biographer presents his return to Ukraine, not as a personal choice, but as the will of God manifested repeatedly through circumstances that made it impossible for Jov to return to Athos. These episodes of Jov's life echo episodes in the lives of the founders of monasticism in Ukraine, Antony and Theodosius, who had also settled where they did, not by self-willed choice, but through God's guidance that made it impossible for them to settle elsewhere.

Once his schooling was finished, Jov, then known as Ivan *Knjahynyc'kyj*, stayed on in the prince's circle, apparently not sure what he wanted to do in life, and in this way he happened to be sent with a gift from the prince to the monks of Mount Athos. There he felt a call to the monastic life and, after settling his affairs in Ukraine, returned to Athos to become a monk. There he lived first as the disciple of an elder, then in a cenobitic community, and finally as a solitary. On a trip to collect alms for his monastery, circumstances detained him in his native region, and he received the blessing of his superiors to remain in Ukraine.

Knjahynyc'kyj intended to lead the life of an anchorite in that region which, with its forests, mountains and many streams, was well suited to the solitary life. Indeed, in those very places and at that time other anchorites were leading just that kind of life. He came into contact with the Balaban family, which he may perhaps already have known as Isaias Balaban was archimandrite of the Univ monastery whose school he had attended. Another Balaban, Gedeon, was bishop of Lviv—as we saw above. It was yet another member of the family, Adam, who provided Ivan with the opportunity he was looking for to retire in solitude to lead a life of prayer.

So it was that Jov began to live as a solitary in Uhornyky and, as often happened when people learn of an anchorite, he began in no time to attract disciples. His manner of living the common life with them, his biographer assures us, soon became known throughout Ukraine.

In a short time Uhornyky was no longer a solitary retreat, and Jov, who desired nothing so much as solitude, after appointing a superior for what was now a flourishing monastic community, went off, seeking a place where he could live 'the very strictest life of stillness'. At about this time he made the acquaintance of a local functionary, Peter Ljaxovyč, who helped him find a place that was indeed solitary, in an unpopulated part of the Carpathians. The place, called Manjava, lay in a remote location of great natural beauty near a stream, with a waterfall nearby, and surrounded by thick forests. There Jov at once made himself a shelter under a tree. Peter Ljaxovyč, who owned some land there, had a cell built for him, and Jov settled down at last to a life of undisturbed prayer in solitude.

This could not last long: for one thing, Jov by this time was too well known and he was soon sought out. First, an elder of the Uhornyky monastery came and asked to be permitted to remain; then Ioan Vyšens'kyj arrived with one of Jov's nephews. Although Vyšens'kyj soon left to return to Athos, others—both monks and seculars—came, entreating Jov to let them stay. Some of them Jov instructed and sent home, others he directed to the cenobitic community at Uhornyky. Only a few did he allow to remain, 'so that the rule of stillness might not be undone'. Not all whom he received remained, so strict was the asceticism practiced by Jov and his disciples.

Although Jov lived with only a few other monks, he still longed for solitude and often retired to a place apart. When he realized that the site of his first cell might be useful to local people for haying and pasturing, his love of solitude and peace led him to transfer his monastery a little further off, to a more inaccessible spot between two small streams. This new place was the site of the Manjava Skete. With the assistance of Peter Ljaxovyč, Jov and his monks built a church in honor of the Exaltation of the Holy Cross. His biographer describes how Jov, who never touched meat or dairy products, prepared meat and cheese for the workers engaged in building the church. By this time the brethren at Manjava numbered eight, and one of them, Theodosius, was soon ordained priest.

Jov had intended that, if disciples must come, at least their number should not surpass twelve, and the church of the Holy Cross was built with that number in view. But the monastic community continued to grow—soon there were forty monks—and a larger church was built.

When Jov made Theodosius superior, he retired to a solitary cell a short distance from the monastery. By that cell was a little church. After his death a small skete, a *skytyk*, was founded on the spot to give other monks of Manjava an opportunity to lead a similar anachoretic life. The four to six monks of the *skytyk* formed a separate small community, dependent on the Manjava cenobium. Their way of life, as reflected in their particular rule, was intended to ensure maximum attention to God.

After Jov's death, Manjava Skete continued. In 1676, during one of the many Tatar invasions of Ukraine, the monastery was besieged and taken, the monks and others who had taken refuge there were killed, and the monastery burned down. Very soon afterwards, however, the monastery was rebuilt and fortified; the iconostasis of its rebuilt church, with the icons painted by the monk-iconographer Jov Kondzelevyč, was among the most outstanding works of religious art of its time.[4] It continued to flourish in its solitude. Besides the *skytyk* described in the writings translated here, another small skete, with a little church of the Ascension, was later built on the mountain top. Throughout the seventeenth and eighteenth centuries all references to the monastery testify to the rigorous asceticism, the tranquil

---

4. Jov Kondzelevyč was a monk of the Bilostok monastery in Volyn', invited by numerous churches to paint icons. After the suppression of Manjava Skete, the iconostasis he painted was transferred to the village church in Bohorodčany; in 1923 it was removed to the National Museum in Lviv.

order, and the beauty of the church services at the Manjava Skete. The end came suddenly and mercilessly. In 1785 emperor Joseph II of Austria suppressed the Manjava Skete, together with other monasteries he considered useless.[5] Jov did not set out to found a monastery. He simply began to live a life that chose as its model the fathers of all christian monasticism, the desert fathers. His was a return to the sources, not by studying them, but by living them. His entire way of life can be summed up in one word, *hesychia*, stillness.

HESYCHASM

The solitary life pursued by Jov, even as a community developed around him, is closely bound up with the spiritual teachings of hesychasm, a word meaning 'absence of noise or speaking' or simply 'stillness'. 'Stillness' is the term I use in translating *bezmolvie*, the slavic word for *hesychia* which incessantly recurs in the texts from Manjava.

'Hesychasm' refers to several closely connected, but distinct, spiritual currents and practices. In its primary meaning, it designates the way of life of the fathers in the egyptian desert who withdrew from the world, that is, ordinary human concerns to live a life of prayer and asceticism based on the Gospels. They lived as anchorites in separate cells, at some distance one from another, although groupings of some cells formed rudimentary communities in which the monks met together at set times for prayer, especially for the Eucharist. They worked with their hands at tasks that did not disturb silent prayer—most often plaiting baskets. They shunned human society, but received hospitably any visitors who might come to them.[6] The withdrawal of the monk from

5. For the history of the Manjava Skete, see Celevyč, who includes many documents in his study.

6. See Russell, and also Helen Waddel, *The Desert Fathers* (London 1936, reprinted many times), an excellent introduction to their way of

human society was conducive to the purification of his heart and his thoughts, the condition for continual prayer, the aim of this way of life.

To aid the habit of prayer a simple form of mental prayer was adopted that prolonged the recitation at set times of the psalms. While the monk engaged in undistracting manual work a brief prayer formula could be repeated in order to fix the mind on God. Eventually the formula to be used most widely was the Jesus Prayer: 'Lord Jesus Christ, Son of the living God, have mercy on me', to which was added later the word, 'a sinner'. The Jesus Prayer eventually became identified with hesychast spirituality.

Later, in the fourteenth century, a method of prayer, consisting basically of controlling the rhythm of one's breathing, was devised as a means to achieve more quickly an awareness of the divine indwelling. This was dubbed a hesychast method of prayer.[7]

Finally, an Athonite monk, who later became archbishop of Thessalonica, Gregory Palamas (c. 1296–1359), developed and systematized a theology that centered on a mystical interpretation of the light seen by the apostles at Christ's transfiguration on Mount Tabor. To this too is given the name of hesychasm.[8]

---

life and spirituality. For a good exposition of the spiritual doctrine of hesychasm, see Pierre Adnès, 'Hésychasme', *Dictionnaire de spiritualité*, 7/1 (Paris 1968) 381–399. It is worth noting that in mss the slavic translation of the collection of apophthegmata of the desert fathers that in Greek carries the conventional title Ἀνδρῶν ἁγίων βίβλος most often bears the title 'Tales of the Holy Elders, How One Should Strive with All One's Might to Attain Stillness '(*bezmolvie*, that is, *hesychia*)'; see Irop єрьомін ' "Своднбий" Патерик у південно-спов' янсъких, українсъкому та московсъкому писъенствах', *Записки Історично-Філологічного відділу Українсъкої Академії Наук*, 12 (1927) 48.

7. See Irénée Hausherr, *La méthode d'oraison hésychaste*, (Orientalia Christiana, 36=IX.2 (Rome: Pontificio Istituto Orientale, 1927).

8. This, of course, vastly simplifies the teachings of Palamas; for an exposition of them, see John Meyendorff, *A Study of Gregory Palamas*,

In the writings from Manjava, hesychasm—or stillness—bears only the first two of the meanings given above: the ancient monks' practice of stillness, in which the Jesus Prayer plays an important role. No trace exists of any physical exercise to promote the Jesus Prayer, nor is there any reference to doctrines that derive from Palamas. Works expounding this method and doctrine appear to have been rather rare in Ukraine, and their direct influence cannot be detected. Many monks from Ukraine, like Jov Knjahynyc'kyj, the founder of Manjava Skete, spent longer or shorter periods on Athos, where the method was practiced and the doctrines propagated. They were doubtlessly acquainted with the hesychast method of prayer and with Palamite doctrines, but perhaps the method was too arcane and the doctrine too speculative to have much meaning in their lives. It is to their particular way of prayer we shall return below in speaking of daily life at Manjava Skete, which aimed at imitating as fully as was possible under different geographical and temporal conditions the hesychasm of the egyptian monks.

The hesychast current in Ukraine did not begin with Manjava, but goes back to the founders of monastic life there, Antony and Theodosius of the Caves. The anachoretism of Antony is a sign of this. Theodosius, after he became the superior of a large community, frequently retired apart, seeking stillness.

Throughout the eighteenth century natural conditions favored a monasticism lived in stillness and solitude. Although Ukraine possessed no impenetrable forests, the Carpathian Mountains and their foothills in western Ukraine as well as the western ukrainian plateau, offered many secluded localities. There caves could be found and adapted for habitations and caves could also be dug out on the high

translated by George Lawrence (Crestwood: Saint Vladimir Seminary Press, 1974). On the usage for the term in this context, see *id.*, 'Is "Hesychasm" the Right Word? Remarks on Religious Ideology in the Fourteenth Century', *Harvard Ukrainian Studies*, 7 (1983) 447–456.

banks of such rivers as the Dnieper or Dniester. The Caves Monastery of Kiev began this way, and in the immediate vicinity of Kiev other caves were used by monks. Still today one can find many caves, especially in western Ukraine, that show clear traces of having been used as monastic habitations.

Cave monasteries by their very nature remained small and solitary. One of the best known of monastic cave complexes in western Ukraine was at Rozhirče on the river Stryj. Here, as in other cave monasteries, the monks took pains to adapt the cave to monastic usage, using one of the caves as a church. Exact dates are impossible to establish, since written records do not exist, but surviving constructional details indicate that this cave monastery arose in the fifteenth century and lasted for a considerable time. In the same region, at the Sataniv Holy Trinity monastery on the river Zbruč, the original cave cells from at least the sixteenth century are still in evidence. Popular tradition connects numerous other caves and solitary localities with monks; in Rozhircče and Sataniv, a skete life in caves can often be traced into the eighteenth century.[9]

Islands, or strips of land in rivers that became islands in full flood, likewise promised seclusion. Finally, when the major Tatar threat passed in the territories east of the Dnieper, this territory, very sparsely settled, attracted monks who desired a peaceful life apart. All regions that offered conditions of separation from populous settlements had a high concentration of monasteries, sketes, and solitary cells.

Solitary cells and sketes sometimes grew into regular cenobia, as did the Dobromyl' monastery mentioned earlier. In the sixteenth century a hieromonk Ananias and a companion built a cell and a small chapel on the slopes of what later came to be called Černeča Hora—Monks' Mountain. In 1613 another small church, of Saint Elias, was built near the

---

9. For further details, see Senyk, 'L'hésychasme'.

peak of the mountain, an indication that by that time other monks were living there in scattered cells. The Dobromyl' monastery continued in this fashion through the seventeenth century. In the last decade of that century, when monastic life in those parts was being reorganized, a large church of Saint Onuphrius and a monastery were built at the foot of the mountain.

Similarly, at the beginning of the seventeenth century, Joel, a monk from Kiev, with a companion Silvester, chose for his cell a wild spot on a hill at a place called Krexiv in western Ukraine. There he chose a cave as his cell and a little higher up built a small church dedicated to Saints Peter and Paul. Soon other monks came to join them. Joel, who liked his solitude, left the church and adjoining space to the small community and for himself built a small chapel over his cave. Yet because the cells of the monks lay too exposed along the path taken by Tatars in their frequent incursions, already in Joel's lifetime the community had to be moved to the other side of the hill. At its new location the monastery was far better protected from the Tatars, but at the same time much more accessible to pious folk from far and near, who began to arrive at the monastery in large numbers even during Joel's lifetime (†1628).

The expansion of Dobromyl' and Krexiv from a solitary cell to a skete took place in the late sixteenth and early seventeenth century, contemporary with the founding of Manjava Skete. In the same years similar foundations abound in all regions of Ukraine. What looks like an increase in numbers may in part reflect only a greater abundance of written sources surviving from this period. Yet there was indubitably a great expansion of monasticism throughout the seventeenth century, and the hesychast current is especially evident. That many monks chose to live as anchorites or in small sketes or in monasteries with a hesychast tradition quite clearly points to an upsurge in hesychast spirituality, even though its sources are not yet clear.

In eastern Ukraine sketes and hermitages were also common in the seventeenth and early eighteenth centuries. Here too anchorites sought out caves on river banks and constructed shelters and simple chapels from wattles. In some parts of eastern Ukraine caves could also be found on wooded rises. Often the course of events was similar: a hermit found and settled in a cave, others soon joined him, and then local people helped in building cells and a church. Monasteries which did not have a hesychast tradition or which, because of changed circumstances, no longer appeared as havens of silence and solitude, very often nevertheless had sketes or hermitages attached to them.

The Kiev Lavra always had some sketes on its properties, at one time scattered throughout Ukraine. Paisij Velyčkovs'kyj was attracted by the stillness of the Kytajiv skete, which had been founded in the early eighteenth century and which he visited a little later while he was a student at the Kiev Academy.[10] Another of the Lavra's sketes near Kiev was at Holosivka, which had cells for nine monks. The Ljubeč monastery when Paisij lived there maintained a small skete of Saint Onuphrius.[11]

When the Dubno Saviour monastery was reformed in 1592, its benefactor, Prince Basil-Constantine Ostroz'kyj, wrote that because some monks might want to live as solitaries in the surrounding woods, he was permitting the monastery to build a skete there.[12] The skete, by its very nature, is seldom mentioned in the sources about the Dubno archimandria, but solitaries were still living there in the second half of the seventeenth century.

The Krexiv monastery—which, as we saw above, began as a hesychast skete—after it had grown in size and became a religious center for the people of the region, maintained a skete for those of its monks who wanted a more solitary

---

10. Featherstone, pp. 8–9.
11. Ibid., p. 31.
12. AJuZR, 6 (Kiev 1883) 93–95.

life. Among their occupations was that of copying manuscripts.

Some monasteries that maintained a hesychast tradition, but outgrew the anachoretic stage, were surrounded by sketes and hermitages. Thus, the Pidhirci monastery maintained a skete by its original church of the Transfiguration. There are examples also of anchorites living apart from, but in dependence on, monasteries.

All these cave monasteries, sketes, and hermits' cells arose from the search for *hesychia*, which is stressed so often in the life of Jov Knjahynyc'kyj, 'who shone forth in the tranquillity of stillness, in his skete by the stream Baters, like Elias and other holy anchorites'. His longing for *hesychia* marks all the stages of his monastic life: on Athos, at Uhornyky, finally at Manjava.

> He rejoiced, because he had obtained the stillness he desired. Ceaselessly he sang the praises of his Master, with the thought of his departure from the body and of Christ's second coming. . . . Ceaselessly his tears flowed. . . . Thus he lived as a solitary, communing only with fear.[13]

When a community developed at Manjava, it was Jov's practice frequently to go off to the 'wilderness' (or 'desert'). In his last years, whenever he could manage it, he remained alone 'in stillness' in his solitary cell and came to the church and the refectory at the monastery only on feast days. Jov's successor, Theodosius, had similar inclinations. Jov's *Life* says that Theodosius persistently asked Jov to be permitted to remain at Manjava 'because he greatly desired the stillness of solitude'.

Seeking stillness was widespread and led many other monks to an anachoretic or a fully eremitical life. The more

---

13. *Life*, sec. 6.

successful they were, the less remains known about them. Occasionally, however, particular circumstances raised one of these monks to prominence, allowing us to give a few examples to show that this striving remained alive in ukrainian monasticism: a monk whom the founder of Manjava Skete knew personally; a contemporary in a distant monastery; and another monk a century later.

The Počajiv monastery, begun at the end of the sixteenth century with a few solitaries living in the woods, soon became, on account of its miraculous icon of the Mother of God, one of the major religious centers in Ukraine. The first superior of Počajiv, Jov Zalizo, had become a monk at Uhornyky shortly after its founding by Jov Knjahynyc′kyj. Jov Zalizo was ordained to the priesthood and received the great schema at Uhornyky. He was then chosen superior of the monastery of the Exaltation of the Holy Cross at Dubno, another Ostroz′kyj foundation, reformed in 1592. Jov Zalizo, who like Jov of Manjava, aspired to a life of *hesychia*, soon resigned his charge at Dubno and retired to Počajiv, at that time a community of only a few anchorites. Not long afterwards he was elected superior and remained in charge over forty years, until his death in 1651.[14] Jov Zalizo sought *hesychia* and as superior of the Počajiv monastery he frequently retired for three days of a week at a time for solitary prayer.

The same quest for stillness and solitude appears prominently in the life of another contemporary of Jov Knjahynyc′kyj, Josaphat Kuncevyč (1580–1623). He was sent

14. See Amvrosij [Lotockij], Сказание о Почаевской Успенской лавре [*Skazanie o Počaevskoj Uspenskoj lavre*] (Počajiv 1878) pp. 23–26, the fullest account of the Počajiv monastery, based on sources. The *Life* of Jov Zalizo written by his disciple Dositheus was published by the monastery in 1791, but the edition is very rare and I have not been able to consult it or the autograph manuscript, which was used by archimandrite Amvrosij in his work and which presumably still exists, although its whereabouts are not certain. Versions of the *Life* that have appeared since the nineteenth century are not reliable and there is no good account in English.

by his father as an apprentice to a merchant in Vilna, where he entered the Holy Trinity monastery. Everyone who knew him agreed in depicting the hesychastic bent of Josaphat. A burgher of Polock gives a typical description.

> As a monk, he became not only a perfect monk, but a real anchorite. All those who used to come to him for the sake of spiritual consolation know from experience that he, to avoid the concourse of men, would shut himself up in the church of the Holy Trinity, and there he spent the whole day either praying or reading spiritual books.[15]

Over a hundred year later Paisij Velyčkovs'kyj (1722–1794), in his wanderings in search for a suitable monastery, met many hesychasts who lived in sketes and hermitages or who, after some years spent in solitude, had returned to a monastery. At the Brotherhood monastery in Kiev the hieroschemonk Paxomij, who encouraged Paisij's attraction to the monastic life by his words and with the writings of the fathers, had spent some years in solitude. Later Paisij came across a hermit living alone, refusing the companionship of even one other monk. In a monastery near the hermit Paisij found an experienced guide, a monk living in a skete in stillness. At the Kiev Lavra, too, he knew monks who had spent some years in solitude.[16] Paisij himself sought the stillness of prayer, although eventually he became the superior of a monastery counting hundreds of monks.

---

15. D. Dorozynskyj, 'Ex actis processus canonizationis gloriosi martyris Josaphat Kuncevicii, Archiep. Polocensis' in Йосиф Сліпий, ed., Св. свщм. Йосафат Кунцевич (Lviv 1925) 196; the same deposition in a latin translation from roman archives can be found in *S. Josaphat Hieromartyr*, ed. Athanasius G. Welykyj, vol. 2 (Rome 1955) 294. See other testimonies in Dorozynskyj, pp. 126, 222–223; SJH 2:223, 322–323. For Josaphat as monk, see S. Senyk, 'The Sources of the Spirituality of St Josaphat Kuncevyč', *Orientalia Christiana Periodica*, 51 (1985).

16. See Featherstone for Paisij's autobiography, esp pp. 7, 44–45, 56.

The Living Tradition of the Fathers

The monks' strong inclination towards anachoretism, the preference for sketes rather than large monasteries, led them to seek inspiration in the examples and writings of hesychast spirituality. Just as they are exhorted to keep the commandments of God, the monks are urged to keep the commandments of the Fathers, because the commandments of the Fathers are in perfect harmony with those of God. Ignatius and Theodosius, the two Manjava authors, constantly cite Scripture; both also appeal to the testimony of the Fathers, whose works the monks read in order to assimilate their teachings.

As a boy Jov liked books and was a good student. This characteristic is common in ukrainian hagiographic and monastic writings. A monk does not invent a way of life, but follows in the footsteps of his predecessors, guided by their example and writings. The teachings of the Fathers, their lives and instruction, are set out in books which the monk reads to make his own. The importance of spiritual reading is also stressed in the lives of Josaphat Kuncevyč and Paisij Velyčkovs'kyj. Josaphat, who had little schooling, knew the Fathers better than many learned theologians did,[17] and Paisij, from his childhood in Poltava until his death, was steeped in them.

The Fathers, like the evangelists and apostles, did not codify their rules, and even the works that bear the title 'Rules', as Saint Basil's, are not monastic rules in a western sense (and the title was not given by Basil). The real rule for the monk is first the teachings of Jesus and of the apostles, to which we shall return below, and then the tradition of the Fathers, a living tradition, handed down through generations, down to 'our father and elder Jov' and one's superior.

---

17. *S Josaphat Hieromartyr,* 1 (Rome 1952) 10.

Strikingly, when Jov decided to withdraw from the community at Manjava, he gave the new superior a volume of the ascetical writings of Saint Basil and exhorted him to regard it 'in place of a rule and to do everything as Basil thought fit'. It may at first seem incongruous that the works of a father as opposed to the solitary life as Saint Basil was should have been singled out by a monk who was on the point of retiring to the anachoretic life. The prominence accorded to Basil by Jov and after him by Theodosius, who cites Basil continuously in his *Testament* is, however, typical of ukrainian monasticism. The reason is the great authority of the archbishop of Caesarea, his central role in all eastern monasticism, and his insistent teaching on the common life. All reforms of monastic life in Ukraine exhort the monks to observe the common life 'according to Saint Basil'.[18] Moreover, several works rejected as clearly inauthentic by modern scholarship were included in the collection of Basil's ascetical writings known in both East and West. These spurious works, discarded from the corpus of Basil's authentic writings, cannot be equally rejected in a study of eastern monasticism, because for many centuries they were read with the attention and esteem given to the works of Basil the Great and their influence was as great as that of his genuine works. They sometimes enlarge upon Basil's teaching and sometimes contradict it—as when they praise the solitary life, which Basil categorically rejected in Long Rule 7 as 'difficult and dangerous'. Thus Jov, going off to his solitary cell, no doubt felt that he had the authority of Basil behind him.

Theodosius, like all eastern monks, anxious to demonstrate that his teaching is not his own, but rests on the authority of the Fathers, frequently refers to his sources. 'I have written nothing of my own,' he says at the beginning of

---

18. To give but one example, see the charter of pr. Ostroz'kyj to the Dubno monastery, 1592, AJuZR, 6:93.

his *Testament*. His writings, like the Life of Jov by Ignatius, are filled with quotations from and allusions to Scripture, especially the Psalms and the New Testament. Theodosius explicitly states that in his *Testament* he is not setting out everything that could be said about the monastic life because the brethren have the writings of the Fathers to instruct them.

Besides Basil, Theodosius cites Ephrem the Syrian, Isaac the Syrian, John Climacus, and Dorotheus of Gaza, as well as *Paterika* and *Gerontika*—that is, the sayings and lives of monastic fathers of various regions: John Cassian, Simeon the New Theologian, Peter Damascene, and Theodore Studite. As might be expected, there are references to the founders of monasticism in Ukraine, Saints Antony and Theodosius of the Caves, and to the *Paterikon* of the Kiev Caves Monastery. Other slavic monastic texts that are named are the writings of Nil' Sorskij and Iosif of Volokolamsk, contemporary representatives of two opposing currents in russian monasticism as regards their way of life, but whose writings converged into the same tradition.

The reference to Nil' Sorskij (1433–1508) is especially important, though not unique in ruthenian monasticism at this period. Josaphat Kuncevyč, as a monk at the Holy Trinity monastery in Vilna, copied out Nil's writings, which means that copies of them were circulating in ruthenian monasteries. Nil', the renovator of the hesychast tradition in russian monasticism, was largely ignored in sixteenth-century Russia; in fact, he came into prominence there again only after Paisij Velyčkovs'kyj revived Nil's writings among his disciples in the latter part of the eighteenth century. That there were monks and monasteries in Ukraine who in the intervening period continued to read and live by Nil's writings is thus noteworthy. The circulation of his works among ukrainian monks indicates an attraction to the hesychast teachings they contain.

The written word—the Scriptures and the Fathers—is all-important for the monks, but concerning themselves they are mute. Theodosius, who quotes the Fathers and who committed his own instructions to writing, nevertheless affirms the need of an authoritative interpreter, the superior, the faithful guardian of tradition.

What I write in my testament needs an inspired teacher, judge, and guardian, and a constant administrator, that is, *ihumen*, a pastor and true leader and superior for the flock, to recall to it God's commandments and my testament according to God. The written word, as one wise man has said, is a dumb philosopher, who understands much, but cannot tell people what he understands. In the same way, writing contains the understanding of many things, but cannot talk of itself. For this it needs a servant and leader, to carry out in deed for the disciples what has been bequeathed, so that the written word may become a salvific deed.[19]

Theodosius constantly corroborates the teachings of the Fathers by the example and teachings of 'our blessed elder and father', Jov. Paisij's comments on readings from the Fathers were an important element of his renewed practice. Paisij was opposed to the publication of the writings he had translated, because he felt that simply reading them, without the guidance of a person experienced in the spiritual life, might bring more harm than good.[20]

HESYCHAST PRAYER

A work contemporary with the Manjava texts thus describes how monks in Ukraine occupy their time in their cells. Prayer

19. *Testament*, final exhortation.
20. See Elia Citterio, 'La scuola filocalica di Paisij Velichkovskij e la *Filocalia* di Nicodimo Aghiorita. Un confronto', *Amore del bello. Studi sulla Filocalia.* (Magnano: Qiqajon 1991) 183–184.

coupled with asceticism is nourished by the works of the Fathers: the Jesus Prayer is singled out.

> They do what the ancient monks in the times of Saint Antony, Theodore, Euthymius, and the other holy Fathers did: some read the psalter, others the holy Gospels, others recite the akathist in honor of the most sweet name of Jesus or of the most holy Virgin and the other saints, begging God for all peoples' and their own salvation. Others recite the Lord's Prayer, the Creed, and the angelic salutation; still others stand all night repeating the brief prayer: *Lord Jesus Christ, Son of God, have mercy on me, a sinner,* by means of which they raise their thoughts to God, in recalling all his benefactions or in examining their consciences. Others yet wear out their bodies in prostrations, while others, sent out or assigned to various services and obediences, submit to Christ himself in the person of their superior. When, after such exertions, they give rest to their bodies . . . they allow them to rest on a poor and very hard mattress or on a mat, some on a bare board or on the ground, for two or three hours, or four at the most. After the night and day prayers, both in church and in the cell, if they have some free time, they read books of the holy Fathers on the monastic way of life, such as Saint Ephrem the Syrian, John Climacus, Isaac the Syrian, Dorotheus, Antioch, and others, which they have in slavic translation from the Greek.[21]

Jov's biographer presents Jov's monastic life from its very beginnings as a pursuit of the conditions required by

---

21. AJuZR, 9 (Kiev 1893) 98 (*Lithos*, an anonymous work, printed in Kiev in 1644)

hesychia. Before Jov, still Ivan, set out for Mount Athos to become a monk there, he settled all his worldly affairs, to begin this new life with a 'mind free from all turmoil', from all preoccupation that might be an obstacle to continual prayer. Solitude was sought as the ideal condition for continual prayer, for the purification of the heart. Jov Knjahynyčkyj achieved this perfect purification and already in this life, as he lay dying, he could join in the unceasing occupation of the angelic hosts: singing the praises of the Most Holy Trinity. The Jesus Prayer, an important component of hesychast spirituality, was a favorite of ukrainian monks. In his *Testament* Theodosius has a long passage on 'mental doing'. In it he says:

> Let us learn unceasing prayer, that is, the remembrance of the name of Jesus. Standing and sitting and lying, in your cell and in the church, at manual work and at table and on the road, continuously in your mind, with your thought or your lips call out: *Lord Jesus Christ, Son of God, have mercy on me, a sinner*. In this way all invasions and entries of extraneous thoughts and assaults will be cut off.[22]

Theodosius here is repeating the teaching of Jov Knjahynyc'kyj.

> He used to say that whoever does not have this prayer continuously and purely in his heart has no arms for combat. He himself throughout his life always kept this prayer, his lips unceasingly moving in repeating it.[23]

---

22. *Testament*, ch 5.
23. *Life*, sec 8.

Jov Zalizo of Počajiv had such great love of silence that, according to his biographer, he was hardly ever heard to speak. About the only thing he could be heard to murmur was, *Lord Jesus Christ, Son of God, have mercy on me.* Josaphat likewise recited the prayer with prostrations 'thousands of times by day and by night, he was so habituated to it that even in his sleep his lips moved with the Jesus Prayer.[24]

These monks were contemporaries, although they came from and lived in different regions. The testimonies about them show that the Jesus prayer was a widespread and favorite practice of ukrainian monks. Yet around the turn of the fourteenth century a hieromonk Paxomij in Priluki in Muscovy wrote to the archimandrite Dosifej of the Kiev Lavra with questions about athonite practices. In his response Dosifej describes the manner of praying the psalter on Athos, then goes on to explain the practice of the Jesus Prayer. He adds that the monks on the Holy Mountain 'for the sake of God in an outstanding manner observe silence and avoid noise and worldly turmoil'.[25] he monks of the Kiev Lavra not only knew of this practice, but followed it themselves, and from then on, if not already earlier, the practice remained alive in ukrainian monasticism. Although the Kiev *Paterikon* mentions this prayer when describing the holy life of Svjatoša, from the family of the Černihiv princes at the beginning of the twelfth century, we cannot be sure it was current then. But it was so from at least the mid-fifteenth century, when the *Paterikon* was edited.[26]

---

24. Jacobus Susza, *Cursus vitae et certamen martyrii B Josaphat Kuncevicii* (Paris 1865) 7. See also Senyk, 'The Sources of the Spirituality of St Josaphat Kuncevyč'.

25. See the letter in Н. Никольский, 'Материалы для истории древнерусской духовной письменности', *Известия Отделения русского языка и словесности.* [N. Nikolskij, 'Materialy dlja istorii drevnerusskoj duxovnoj pismennosti', *Izvestija Otdelenija russkogo jazyka i slovesnosti]* 8 (1903), no. 2:65–68.

26. See *The Paterik,* trans. Heppell, p. 132. On the Jesus Prayer in eastern monastic tradition, see especially Irénée Hausherr, *The Name of Jesus,*

Good order, the preservation of orderliness 'in church and in the refectory', are phrases that are constantly repeated in the Manjava texts. Without knowing Saint Augustine's definition of peace as the 'tranquility of order', the authors express the same idea. An ordered way of life in common prayer, in work, in the gatherings of the community, a way according to rule, prevents disorder and its tumult, noise. It serves to preserve peace among the brethren and the tranquility that is a necessary condition for continual prayer. The good order constantly recommended by Theodosius preserves hesychia.

Hesychasm, provided the basic direction and determined how other aspects of monastic life were to be lived concretely at Manjava. Along with hesychasm, Jov Knjahynyc'kyj impressed on his foundation a return to certain fundamental practices of monasticism too often neglected in the East.

The Reform Effected by Manjava

Stability

A temptation endemic to eastern monasticism is the itch to roam through the world. This temptation is also known in western monasticism—one need only recall the peregrinations of the early irish monks. In the West, however, the *stabilitas* demanded by the Rule of Saint Benedict in the long run put an end to the wandering of monks. Eastern monasticism knew no generally imposed rule having canonical force; the rules and writings of the Fathers had only moral authority. Enactments of church councils and sporadic civil laws were not compellingly applied. As a result, monks, and to a lesser extent nuns, roamed at will. At times, there were good reasons: to pass to a better organized monastery, to seek out

---

translated Charles Cummings, CS 44 (Kalamazoo: Cistercian Publications, 1978).

an experienced spiritual father. The bulk of testimony about these roving monastics, however, makes it clear that for most part the motive was escape from the burdens of monastic obedience and monastic work. Complaints from all ages and places speak of monks going about aimlessly, settling briefly in a place, and, when easy provision for a life without toil could no longer be had there, moving on to another.

The texts from Manjava frequently speak of the spiritual benefits of staying in one monastery. Their authors knew how ingrained was the habit of going from monastery to monastery and how strong an attraction the example of wandering monks exerted. Theodosius repeatedly pleads with his monks to resist that temptation and to remain at Manjava. The author of Jov's *Life* is at pains to explain that the elder left his monastery not because he grew tired of staying in one place, but because God so arranged his life, and describes Jov's repeated attempts to return to the monastery in which he had been professed. It is to counteract the *wanderlust* of monks that Ignatius writes: 'if someone ends his life in the same monastery where he was tonsured, even if he had not observed unusually great *podvyhy*, such a monk will unfailingly be crowned'. He knew well, in fact, that for many monks stability was a greater *podvyh*, than physical austerities, requiring a greater spiritual effort and resistance to temptation.

Common Life

A monastic life without stability, with monastics roaming at will, cannot be expected to maintain a high standard of common life. An absence of common life, in fact, is one of the ills of eastern monasticism, in all countries and at all periods. The neglect of common life even acquired a tacitly recognized respectability. On Mount Athos an idiorrhythmic way of life had spread already in the fourteenth century and soon became dominant. The monks disposed of their work for their individual maintenance, owned property, and prepared and took their meals in their cells.

In spite of the acceptance of idiorrhythmia as a monastic way of life, all monastic reformers insist on the preservation or, far more often, the restoration of common life. This applies to the monastic revival in Ukraine in the seventeenth century, even though it was the work mainly of monks with a marked inclination for the solitary life.

In writings of that period, such as those from Manjava, wherever mention is made of common life, this always refers not to life in a cenobium, as opposed to life in a hermitage, but to a community of life, whether with one companion, with several, or with a great number. It refers not only to a common table and church services in common, but also to a common distribution both of work and of all necessary provisions. The monk, whether working with others or alone, gives his work over to his superior; he receives no individual pay or goods, but only what he needs from the common stores.

These remarks may seem to belabor the obvious. In the East, however, they are far from superfluous. The frequent reiteration in the writings translated here that Manjava Skete follows the common life, the pressing exhortations to the brethren to preserve common life, the stress laid on incidents in Jov's life that demonstrate his perfect observance of the ideals of common life are all meant to counteract the example of many other monasteries where common life was not practiced. As in teachings on poverty what is all important is the interior attitude of refusing the allure of comforts or possessions, so with the common life, it is the interior disposition of loving one's neighbor as oneself and refusing all personal advantage. Jov Knjahynyc'kyj, therefore, can be held up as a model of observance of common life even when he was living in a solitary cell on Athos at the beginning of his monastic life or in a solitary cell, shared only by one brother-monk, at Manjava at his life's end.

When the first companions came to Jov Knjahynyc'kyj, 'soon the fame of his common way of life spread through all Rus'. It was to reform—or revive—common life that Jov was invited to Univ, to Derman', to the Kiev Lavra itself. His biographer describes Jov's practice at Manjava, after first speaking of his exhortations to mutual love.

> He himself did nothing without first proposing it and seeking the counsel of those who lived with him, all of them being of one mind. He did this not because he did not know what to do, but out of respect for his neighbor and because, as he said, such is the order of common life and this is what it means to be of one mind, according to Saint Basil. He had such a high regard for a community of love that nothing was put out to eat or to drink in the refectory unless there was enough for everyone;if it did not suffice for everyone, he would by no means allow it to be served.[27]

Already on his deathbed, when the monks brought him some food and told him, 'we made this especially for you', he refused to touch it because, living in his cell with a fellow-monk, he shared with him everything equally.

At the *skytyk* of Manjava, which was intended to provide the greatest possible solitude, the monks came together for the office and meals, and the *Rule* for the *skytyk* likewise emphasizes common life. Life in a cenobitic monastery and the pursuit of *hesychia* are often regarded and indeed often are opposed to each other. The hum of affairs in a cenobium, however well-ordered and however muted, and the seeking of maximum solitude and quiet, do not easily coexist, but the two were reconciled at the Manjava Skete.

---

27. *Life*, sec 8.

In his *Testament* Theodosius explains the uniting of hesychasm and cenobitism as observed in Manjava.

Our holy monastery combines both ways of life,
namely, the apostolic common life and ascetic
anachoretism in stillness and solitude. This is
because many, both earlier and now, desire and
begin that utter stillness and anachoretism, for the
sake of pure prayer, then, because of the weakness
of our nature and the austerity of that way of
life and lack of necessities, or rather, because of
the small faith and the infirmity of this present
generation, abandon it without having achieved
anything. Others choose to live in common, that
is, together with many brethren, for the sake of
having what is required for the needs of the body.
But in its tumult and cares they completely lose
their mettle and are overcome by lusts, and all the
passions come alive in them . . .

But this holy skete community combines both
kinds of life taught by the fathers. I beg you,
therefore, fathers and brethren and holy children,
strive to carry out all the observances of common
life, in the good order in the church and in the
refectory, finding joy in the common singing and
church services, the beauty of the holy church and
of the sacred vestments and vessels, as also in a
moderate table, with continence. The rest of your
bodily requirements, in moderation, you have
from God: clothing and shoes, food and drink.
Above all, you have the benefit and consolation
of a holy and good companionship, brethren who
are of the same inclinations and share the same
podvyhy. Those also who live according to the
second way, in asceticism, solitude, and stillness,
keep the anachoretic way of life and silence of the

lips. Everywhere, in the cell and at manual work and outside the monastery, preserve silence and attentiveness, I beg you, with the remembrance of Jesus.[28]

In the following century Paisij Velyčkovs'kyj, asked by a friend in Poltava to describe his manner of life with the community at Dragomirna, responded in similar terms. He too spoke of the combining of the way of solitary stillness with the way of the common life, both of which are based on the teachings of the fathers.[29]

At Manjava it was also possible for an experienced monk who had lived in community for many years to retire as a solitary, either for a time (whether a set period or indefinitely) or for life. But even in this case the ties of common life were not broken: the monastery supplied the solitary with food, and he in his prayers nurtured the bonds of charity with his brethren.

The *Life* of Jov describes how, as the monastic life instituted at Manjava became known, its founder was asked to help in reforming other monasteries, even the Kiev Lavra itself. The element that raised Jov's foundations—first at Uhornyky, then at Manjava—above most other monasteries of its time was the insistence on a strict observance of common life. The existence of numerous solitaries and the relative freedom of passing, even often, from one monastery to another are among the causes that throughout the East weakened a sense of the cenobium and even canonized idiorrhythmia, an uncenobitic way of life. All three works from Manjava are conspicuous by their insistence on the common life, whether observed in the large monastic community, in the small skete, or in the cell in which Jov lived with one other monk.

---

28. *Testament*, ch. 6.
29. Featherstone, 152.

Common Life and the Gospel

Jov prayed that the 'evangelical christian life' might be renewed in Ukraine, 'a common life lived according to Christ's
commandments'. This definition of monasticism underlines
the Gospel roots of monasticism, which is nothing else but a
radical following of Christ.

Repeatedly common life is called 'evangelical and apostolic': the Gospels together with the *Apostol* (the slavic name
for the book of Acts and the Epistles) are the fundamental
rule of life of all Christians, but especially of monks. The
Gospels describe the life led in common by the Twelve with
their Master, and the Acts and the Epistles give further
examples and directives. As Theodosius proclaims at the
beginning of his *Testament*, the Gospels and the *Apostol* are
the foundation of monastic life. The life led by the Manjava
monks, hence, is apostolic, since it imitates the life of the
Apostles, both during the time when they had Jesus with
them and afterwards, when they were forming the first christian communities. This use of the term 'apostolic' is ancient;
Palladius praises his teacher, the noted monk and spiritual
author Evagrius (†399), for having led an 'apostolic' life.[30]
This usage may astonish western readers, who are more accustomed to seeing 'apostolic' applied to active missionary
and pastoral work. This too is an imitation of the Apostles,
sent out after Pentecost. The monk, however, leads the life of
an apostle with Jesus still present, listening to his teachings
and imitating his mode of life.

Common life, as instituted in Manjava, did not mean
only sharing all material goods. This sharing, in fact, can
be achieved only because there is a community of spiritual
goals and agreement on how to pursue them, in other words,
because there is among all the brethren 'only one heart and
one soul', as in the first community of believers in Jerusalem.

---

30. Palladius, *Lausiac History*, ch. 38; see Cuthbert Butler, *The Lausiac
History of Palladius*, 2 (Cambridge 1904) 116.

Saint Basil, at the very beginning of what came to be called
his Long Rules, underlines this common intent and concord.
The description of the Jerusalem community and Basil's
depiction of what a monastic community should be are
the two sources on which Theodosius of Manjava draws
when he repeatedly stresses that the brethren of Manjava
are to observe the evangelical common life. Like Saint Basil,
Theodosius frequently recalls Acts 4:32.

The same emphasis on common life is given by Jov's
biographer, Ignatius. When Jov settled at Uhornyky the
ktytor, Adam Balaban, voiced the hope that like-minded
brethren might join him. The insistence on common life
determined that the office was celebrated in common, even
at the *skytyk*, contrary to the practice of other anchorites.

Common life understood in this way is a life of christian
love. When disciples began to settle at Manjava, Jov taught
them the outstanding mark of Christ's disciples, to love one
another, and he built up a community of love. Similarly, his
follower Theodosius, when he set down his teaching, began
with charity; this charity then flows over on all other people.
Jov preferred to have the first church built not immediately
by the cells, but at a small distance, where it would still
be accessible to the monks, but would also serve travelers
in those parts, where there were not many settlements and
hence few churches. He moved the cells themselves when
he realized that the land on which they stood might lead to
contention on the part of the local population.

LIFE AT MANJAVA

The Manjava Skete was built after the pattern of most
ukrainian monasteries. Because it was located on a hillside,
by a stream, the monastic enclosure was of irregular shape.
Originally a simple wooden palisade ran around it, but in
the late seventeenth century a stone wall with towers was
raised for protection against Tatar attacks.

The main monastery church always stood in the center of such an enclosure. We see this also at the Uhornyky monastery: Jov's *Life* describes how the *ktytor* of the Uhornyky monastery intended to build a stone church in the middle of the enclosure, but died before carrying out his proposal. In the center of the Manjava Skete stood the church of the Holy Cross, built of wood. It had the plan of a greek cross, with rounded corners of the south, north, and east arms. Around the sides of the enclosure ran the cells of the monks, simple wooden cabins, and the common buildings, also built of wood: kitchen, refectory, storerooms.

Monastic profession

The benefactor who gave Jov the land on which the Uhornyky monastery was built told Jov that his only task was simply to be a monk, *spasajsja*. The word comes from the verb 'to save' (*spasaty*), used reflexively. It means more than 'be saved'; it signifies an activity, an active striving after salvation, hence, roughly, 'work out your salvation', 'strive for your salvation'. Such a translation, however, does not exhaust the term's meaning. *Spasatysja*—working at one's salvation—is often used as a synonym for the monastic life. The origins of this usage go back to the desert fathers. The apophthegmata abound with persons coming to the great elders with variations of the question: 'What shall I do to be saved?'[31] The monastic life, from its origins was undertaken with this one end in view, to save one's soul. The Ascetical Prologue which generations of monks read as the work of Saint Basil declares categorically in its opening words: 'The ascetical life has only one goal, the salvation of the soul'.[32]

The descriptions of Jov's life and of life at Manjava manifests the stages of all monasticism in the byzantine

---

31. See e.g., the question posed to Macarius the Great, in the alphabetical series, Macarius the Egyptian, 23, PG 65:272.

32. Baguenard, p. 45 (Prologue V; Clarke, p. 141, Wagner, p. 217); as the note there points out, Basil himself put the goal somewhat differently.

tradition. A candidate accepted into a monastery becomes a novice, *poslušnyk*, which literally means 'an obedient'. Neither for the novitiate nor for any other stage of monastic profession is there a set period; the candidate passes on if he has the desire and if the superior and his spiritual father consider him ready for it. A novice may be given the habit, *rjasa*; he is then outwardly indistinguishable from a professed monk. Jov, after he had spent a year and a half on Athos under the direction of the hieromonk Isidore, was given the *rjasa*, but remained a novice, *poslušnyk*, and, in fact, was sent to the Vatopedi community to continue his monastic formation.[33]

The monastic tonsure of the small angelic habit (*microschema*) is the equivalent of profession in western monasticism; it involves receiving the tonsure and a change of name, and being vested with the mantle. Monks and nuns advanced in years and spiritual proficiency may assume the great angelic habit (*megaloschema*, in slavic usually simply *sxyma*); this entails greater asceticism and withdrawal for the sake of prayer and often a second change of name. Thus the founder of Manjava Skete was baptized John (Ioan in Church Slavic); when he was given the small habit, his monastic profession, he received the name Ezechiel, and only at the great habit did he assume the name Jov, by which he is known to posterity. Theodosius too assumed the great schema, apparently shortly before he died and without a change of name; in the superscription of his *Testament* he is called hieroschemonk Theodosius, which means a priestmonk with the great schema.

The Vows

Because eastern theology does not make a distinction between evangelical precepts and counsels, eastern monastics

---

33. *Life*, sec 3.

do not profess three specific vows, but vow to remain in the monastic state until their death and to observe its precepts. The monastic vows of the benedictine tradition—obedience, conversion of life, and stability—and three vows of religious life in the West—obedience, chastity, and poverty—are included in such a profession, of course, and obedience and chastity are understood in the same way as in the West. Poverty, however, needs some comment.

'Poverty' is not a category in eastern spirituality, but a number of specific terms designate the plainness and lack of material comforts in a monastic's life as well as the spirit of unacquisitiveness that gives the outward circumstances spiritual value. The accent is on a real poverty in clothing, in food, in dwelling, in all the material surroundings of the monastic's life. The monastic not only lives in poor conditions, but he does not hanker after better; he is satisfied with a minimum of material goods. This is what Theodosius strives to instill when he writes in his *Testament* that the monks should be content with the skete's plain fare, with simple and coarse and perhaps worn clothes.

Spiritual Direction

The superior is the living voice of monastic tradition for the community. In addition, the personal spiritual life of each monk needs the guidance of an experienced and spiritually enlightened father.

The practice and teaching on spiritual direction are not set out in the writings from Manjava, but many allusions to them show the importance attached to the manifestation of thoughts, *logismoi*.[34] Jov Knjahynyc'kyj was a spiritual father before he became superior. After a community had

---

34. On the practice of manifesting one's thoughts to one's spiritual father, see the excellent study, one of the best on eastern spirituality, by Irénée Hausherr, *Spiritual Direction in the Early Christian East*, trans. Anthony P. Gythiel, CS 116 (Kalamazoo: Cistercian Publications, 1990).

been formed at Manjava, monks from other monasteries continued to come to him, to confess to him their thoughts; among them was Theodosius. As soon as Theodosius, by then already a member of the Manjava community, was ordained priest, immediately Jov 'committed all the brethren to him as their spiritual father'. Several times Jov's *Life* refers to Theodosius as the spiritual father of all the monks, even of Jov himself.

This point needs to be examined a little. Spiritual father-hood is a charism that does not require priestly orders; the office of superior in eastern monasticism likewise does not require the priesthood. There exists, however, a profound esteem of the spiritual dignity of priests, a current going back to the desert fathers and also to John Chrysostom. Like Saint Francis of Assisi in the West, Jov did not become a priest because he possessed this exalted sense of priestly dignity coupled with a deep sense of his own unworthiness.

> The elder indeed always held those in orders in honor. When a priest, be he monk or a secular priest, came to him, [Jov] always bowed before him and kissed his right hand. If a deacon came, he honored him by asking him to recite a prayer and he too, like Saint Antony, had his disciple, a deacon, do this.[35]

In such a milieu, a monk found worthy of being ordained priest could not be other than someone possessing as well the qualifications needed to be the spiritual father and the superior of others. Theodosius became spiritual father by reason of his priesthood and in his own *Testament* he recommends that the superiors of Manjava Skete be always chosen from among the hieromonks.

---

35. *Life*, sec 12.

Prayer

The daily routine in all christian monasticism is set by the canonical hours. There is, however, a notable difference in the praying of the Office in East and West. In the Orthodox tradition Vespers, Matins, and the four little hours are church services and require for their celebration the presence of a priest ; Compline and the midnight office are also often celebrated in a church with a priest officiating, but may be prayed privately in one's cell.

As we have already noted, Jov Knjahynyc'kyj was never ordained. When he lived as a solitary, and even when, at Manjava, disciples began to gather around him, there was no priest until the ordination of Theodosius. Without a priest, Jov and the other monks prayed in common, not the church offices, but a 'rule', that is, a set compilation of psalms and of prayers from the Office, generally with prostrations. In the sense in which 'liturgical' is used in the West, this 'rule of prayer' is as liturgical as the Office proper.

In addition, every monk in his cell recited an individual prayer rule; this prayer rule varies from monastery to monastery. This rule of prayer is set out in the *Rule* for the *skytyk*; an abbreviated and less demanding version of the rule was observed by the other monks in the monastery proper. The Jesus Prayer, besides being prayed silently, 'sitting and standing and lying', all through the day, also formed part of the prayer rule. It was said a certain number of times, usually several hundred, a day and counted on a rosary. In the *skytyk* three hundred prostrations were to accompany the recitation of this prayer, but in the monastery the rule probably required prostrations only with the first and last ten or so Jesus Prayers.

The *Rule* for the *skytyk* gives the daily schedule, which in outline was followed also at the main monastery. The monks rose before dawn to recite the midnight office in their cells; Matins and the first hour in common followed.

Private prayer, with an emphasis on the Psalter and the Jesus Prayer with prostrations and with spiritual reading lasted until the time for the third and sixth hours, again in common. If there were two meals that day, the main meal was then taken. Afterwards, the monks went about their tasks: either common works for the community or manual work in their cells. The ninth hour was said with Vespers which was followed by the evening meal, if there were two that day. If there was only one meal, it was taken between the ninth hour and Vespers. In the *skytyk*, where there was regularly only one meal, it was taken between the ninth hour and Vespers. Compline marked the end of the day. The monks then retired to their cells to continue their personal prayer, perhaps to do a little undisturbing manual work. As everywhere in monasteries, eastern and western, the time from Compline until the end of Matins the next day was a time of total silence, for the sake both of recollection and of rest.

In the East, 'liturgy' means the eucharistic liturgy. Until the Manjava Skete acquired its first priest in the person of Theodosius, the liturgy there was celebrated only occasionally by visiting clergy, as the *Life* of Jov informs us. In the East, the eucharistic liturgy is the culmination of all other church services, but because it is, it is not regarded apart from the other services, which are considered a preparation for it. The absence of the Eucharist in the life of those who lead a solitary life is practically a consequence of that way of life. Jov longed for a regular celebration of all church services, especially of the Eucharist. But Jov, for all his desire to have the Eucharist regularly, told Theodosius, to test him, that there was no place among anchorites for a person dedicated to serving the altar. 'We don't have a church, since anchorites seek out not churches, but to purify and save their souls in silence and weeping.'[36]

The texts say nothing about the frequency of the *Eucharist* at the Manjava Skete once the community grew and some

---

36. *Life*, sec 9.

of the monks were priests. If analogies are drawn from other ukrainian monasteries of that period, the Eucharist was celebrated daily by the hieromonks in turn, but it was attended only by those assigned to sing the responses, also in turn by groups, and by those otherwise free from chores and who wished to attend. Only on Sundays and feasts did the entire community participate.[37] At the *skytyk*, as we learn from the *Rule*, the Eucharist was celebrated only once or twice a week, if there were hieromonks to celebrate it.

In the *Rule* for the *skytyk* we find a notable divergence from the normal practice of byzantine monasticism: the monks of the *skytyk* are not to sing the Office, but only to recite it. Only the eucharistic liturgy was to be sung, if the monks of the *skytyk* were able to sing it. This proviso is due not to practical reasons arising from their small number and perhaps an absence of singers, but to the basic direction of the *skytyk* and of Manjava Skete as a whole.

The byzantine Offices are much lengthier than their western counterparts, and in monasteries of any size the monks take turns in chanting them, according to the specific arrangement in each monastery. In small sketes, on the other hand, there was usually no daily Office in common. In Manjava, however, the stress on common life led also to regular common prayer from the very beginnings, as we see in Jov's *Life*. This rule was to be perpetuated even at the *skytyk*. Thus, even the cook, who is ordinarily dispensed from participating in much of the Office, at the *skytyk* was to take part equally with the rest. To unite the requirements of an Office in common and work, an obligation that likewise rested on all the monks, some way had to be found to lighten the office. This could have been achieved in several ways. The curtailment of singing accorded with the simplicity and asceticism of the monks and was conducive to the atmosphere of contemplative prayer that reigned at the *skytyk*.

---

37. Cf. S. Senyk, 'The Eucharistic Liturgy in Ruthenian Church Practice', *Orientalia Christiana Periodica*, 51 (1985) 123–155.

Fasting

An important component of life at Manjava was an asceticism pursued seriously as a necessary prerequisite for any life of prayer, as the very condition for purifying the heart from passions. The liturgical rule of monasteries also determined the fasts. The directives on fasting in the *Testament* and the *Rule* are traditional, although more severe than those in many other monasteries of their time.

Fasting in the East means abstaining not only from meat, but also from eggs and dairy products; fish too is generally excluded from a fast diet. Manjava Skete, like everyone else—monastics and laity—observed this on all fast days and in fast seasons. Like all monastics, the monks of Manjava never ate meat, but they went further, abstaining perpetually also from dairy products. In the *skytyk* there was never even any fish; its monks had fish only when they visited the main cenobium. On fast days, moreover, the dishes were not seasoned with oil. This is the xerophagia, literally, 'dry food', a form of abstinence common in the East. Furthermore, on fast days, especially in the four fast seasons, there was only one meal a day, as was the practice of ancient monks.

Rigorous though the fasts were, the texts make it clear that they were not pursued with rigorism. Fasting is a means, not an end in itself. The superior could mitigate the community fast on account of heavy work. The sections on fasting in the Testament show also a concern for individual needs—the sick, of course, but also those allergic to certain foods and those with other needs.

Work

Prayer for the monk consists not only in the recitation of set Offices; it is his continual occupation. But the monk, like every other human being, also has the obligation to work;

'singing continually the praises of God',[38] the monk went about his work. At Manjava, at both skete and *skytyk*, there were tasks that needed to be done for the community as a whole: the care of the church, preparing firewood, cooking, baking, looking after provisions. All the monks not occupied with these tasks were to spend their time, when they were not engaged in prayer in church or in their rule in the cell, at *rukodilie*, which I translate in the texts as manual work, although its meaning is narrower than manual work, yet broader than handicrafts. *Rukodilie* refers to work that can be done sitting in one's cell and that does not require mental concentration, and so is conducive to recollection and mental prayer. At Manjava, as the texts show, the monks carved crosses, made wooden spoons or woolen garments. These items were sold by the monastery, sometimes to visitors, and monks were regularly sent with them to market.

Some monks with a skill for it copied liturgical and spiritual books. Although in the West by the early seventeenth century printing had well-nigh displaced the copyist, in Ukraine and other lands of eastern Christianity printing presses were as yet few and their production inadequate to supply the demand for books. In addition, printed books were very costly. At Manjava Skete, as in other ukrainian monasteries of the seventeenth century, even the full set of books required for the community services was acquired only over a long period of time. For a full celebration of the byzantine Office, in fact, very many volumes are needed. Books for the Eucharist and for the Office at Manjava as in other ukrainian monasteries, therefore, continued to be copied by hand into the nineteenth century. Although it was time-consuming, it was cheaper to copy books than to buy printed editions, even if these were available. For this reason, however, a second community, such as the *skytyk* at Manjava,

---

38. *Life*, sec. 8.

was even less likely to have a full set of office books; this is reflected in the directions Theodosius gives about the Office (no. 2 of the *Rule*).

There were also few printed editions of slavic translations of the Fathers. Monastery libraries of those times had mostly manuscript copies of the Fathers, especially in anthologies of favorite texts. This copying too, of additional copies or of a manuscript borrowed from some other monastery, occupied some monks. In this respect Manjava Skete did not differ from other ruthenian, russian, and balkan monasteries. Ignatius tells us that Jov was a skilled copyist, and this probably means that Ignatius had occasion to see samples of Jov's copying, done either when he lived alone or when a community had already begun to form around his cell.

The superior, *ihumen*, of the Skete was first of all the spiritual father of the monks. The administration of the material side was overseen by the *econome*. The *econome* saw to the general state of the buildings, the stores of provisions, selling the handwork of the monks and buying what the monastery needed. He was assisted, as the monastery grew in size, by persons with more specific charges, such as the cellarer, whose duty it was to look after the food stores: to see that enough was on hand, especially for the long winters, that it was properly stored, that things were not spoiling. Another monk was in charge of the wardrobe. There was a cook, a monk charged with baking bread, a monk who took care of the refectory and put out the bread and water at mealtimes.

The Testament and the Rule reveal some details of the common life as it was lived. Clothes were kept in a common wardrobe and given out according to season. Every winter, for instance, sheepskin coats were distributed to the monks. Each year only one or two of these coats were new, and Theodosius counsels his monks not to be eager to obtain a new garment, but to be content with the old and worn.

Some local ukrainian customs are reflected. Theodosius

writes, for instance, about a meal in commemoration of a deceased monk. This is the *tryzna*, a custom going back to pre-christian times, but the meal originally in honor of dead ancestors becomes a christian *agape*, no longer looking back, in honor of shades, but looking forward, towards the general resurrection and the marriage feast of the Lamb.

THE INFLUENCE OF MANJAVA

Jov's *Life* reports how he was asked at various times to assist in the reform of existing monasteries, Univ, Derman', the Kiev Lavra. The desire within the monastic world itself to improve its way of life—although not shared by all monks, as we also learn from the Life—is a sign of vitality. Other contemporary sources bear out this picture. At Derman' the *ktytor*, prince Basil Ostroz'kyj, placed another monk who had lived on Athos, Isaac Boryskovyč, as superior and recommended that the rule of Saint Basil be followed.[39] As has already been mentioned, such a recommendation, frequent in the monastic writings of this period, always had one aim in view: a perfect observance of common life, one of the chief teachings of the ascetic works of Saint Basil.

Manjava's example had salutary effects not only on the monasteries mentioned in the texts. Jov's teachings and the manner of life he introduced were carried to other monasteries by his monks from Uhornyky and Manjava, as well as by those monks of other monasteries who came to spend shorter or longer periods of time with him. Like so many other features of Jov's life, this too reminds us of the way that later the influence of Paisij Velyčkovs'kyj spread throughout the slavic and romanian East. Jov's influence continued unabated after his death.

---

39. *Памятники, изданные Временною коммиссиею для разбора древних актов* [*Pamjatniki, izdannye Vremennoju kommissieju dlja razbora drevn:x aktov*, 4 (Kiev 1859) 34–38.

Uhornyky, Jov's first monastery, remained closely tied to Manjava throughout the seventeenth century. Other monasteries adopted The Skete rule or became associated with Manjava. The Pidhirci monastery, in the hilly region between Lviv and Počajiv, has already been mentioned. Local tradition reports monks here already in pre-mongolian times, that is, before 1240, but the monastery chronicle begins its history only from the second half of the sixteenth century.[40]

A certain native of that region as a young man went to Athos, where he became a monk at the lavra of Saint Athanasius; after some time he returned to Pidhirci to live as a solitary in a cave he had dug. There he remained for forty-five years, until his death in 1625, without companions, but sought out by many people for spiritual counsel. After his death, his cave was occupied by two or three monks at a time. In 1659 a monk of Manjava, who had stopped to see some relatives nearby, was attracted by this peaceful location and began to live there; soon he was joined by another monk from Manjava. Before they began to form a monastic community they asked the blessing of the other fathers of Manjava and adopted the skete way of life, 'as it is written in the *Paterikon* of the blessed father Jov and Theodosius', that is, as it is set out in Jov's *Life* and in the *Testament* and *Rule* of Theodosius. Pidhirci soon became an important center of monastic life and had an influence on other monasteries, in this way disseminating the traditions of Manjava.

Manjava's example continued to influence older monasteries as well. The Saint Onuphrius Monastery in Lavriv, also in the Carpathian Mountains, whose origins went back to the fourteenth century, adopted the Manjava rule in 1659. Throughout the seventeenth century numerous monasteries

---

40. The Pidhirci monastery chronicle was published by J. Skruten', 'Сінопсис пліснесько-підгорецького монастиря' [Sinopsys plisnes'ko-pidhorec'koho monastyrja'], *Analecta OSBM*, 1, no.1 (1924) 92–103; no. 2–3 (1925) 306–313; no.4 (1927) 580–591; 3, no.1 (1928) 156–164; the publication was not completed.

in all parts of Ukraine were founded or developed out of the cells of solitaries. In western Ukraine especially, many of them adopted the rule of Manjava, with its strict observance of the common life and its other customs. Superiors were elected annually, 'according to the customs of the Skete'.

Monks from Manjava became the founders of other sketes. Since most ukrainian sketes remained small and never achieved prominence, it is often difficult to trace their history, and so to determine how many owed their origins to Manjava. Only by way of exception are we informed that the monasteries of Tokmačyk and Kolomyja were founded by Manjava monks around the middle of the seventeenth century.[41]

Indeed, almost from the first years of its existence the Manjava Skete came to be looked on as a model of monastic life to such a degree that it was referred to simply as *Skyt*, *The* Skete. Jov's prayer for the restoration of monastic life was amply answered.

The Manjava Skete was a spiritual beacon as well to the general population, primarily within, but also beyond, its immediate region. The *Life* and the *Testament* both mention persons in the world who came there seeking spiritual nourishment; as their confessors and spiritual directors the people preferred monks over the secular clergy. This stream of people continued even after the parishes in the vicinity, along with the entire diocese, accepted church union with Rome in 1700, while Manjava Skete remained Orthodox. Large numbers of pilgrims came to Manjava on feasts, especially on the Exaltation of the Holy Cross, the title of the Skete's main church.[42] They were drawn by the monastery's spiritual atmosphere and the church services sung by the monks. Pastors in the Dniester river region in 1746 were reminded to admonish their parishioners not

---

41. See Celevyč, pp. 51–53, and further examples there.

42. Celevyč, *passim*, provides many instances of the spiritual influence of Manjava on the surrounding population.

to go to Manjava Skete, especially to make their Easter confession.

Manjava's importance, however, goes beyond such direct influence on monasteries and layfolk. The strict rule and the hesychast spirituality of Manjava Skete—both features based on the teachings of the Fathers—demonstrate that these teachings had been kept alive in ukrainian monasticism. They correct a superficial impression of unmitigated monastic decline, not only in sixteenth-century, but also in seventeenth and eighteenth century monastic life in Ukraine. In the latter part of the eighteenth century the reform movement that was inspired by Paisij Velyčkovs'kyj, as far as Ukraine goes, did not arise in a total wasteland, but was linked to a still living tradition, out of which, indeed, Paisij himself came.

This can be demonstrated by the texts of the Fathers quoted by Ignatius and especially by Theodosius. Writings that in the late eighteenth century entered the slavic *Philocalia*, the *Dobrotoljubie*—such as those of Isaac the Syrian— were well known at Manjava. Many citations from Isaac contained in the *Testament* of Theodosius are found in the selections from Isaac included in the *Dobrotoljubie*.[43]

Some of Theodosius' citations of the Fathers that are difficult to trace are found also in the fourteenth-century greek writings on hesychasm of Saint Gregory of Sinai and of Callistus (later patriarch of Constantinople, †1360) and of Ignatius of Xanthopoulos, writings that in the eighteenth century were included in the *Philocalia* of Nicodemus of the Holy Mountain and in its slavic counterpart, *Dobrotoljubie*. Perhaps Theodosius picked up these passages not directly from the Fathers he cites, but through fourteenth-century authors whom he does not name. If this hypothesis can be accepted, we would have evidence that the important writings on hesychast prayer of Gregory of Sinai and of the

---

43. On the greek and slavic versions of the *Philocalia*, see the collection of studies, *Amore del bello* (Magnano: Qiqajon, 1991).

two Xanthopoulos monks were already forming monks in Manjava, and in other ukrainian monasteries, in the first part of the seventeenth century. This would demonstrate once again that the Paisij Velyčkovs'kyj's work of translation was the continuation of a tradition in Ukraine. The way of life that Paisij's biographer Mytrofan describes as existing in the monastic communities under Paisij's direction in Moldavia, in Dragomirna, Secu, and Neamtč, and the spirit that prevailed there are strikingly similar to that of the Manjava Skete.[44] Both Jov and Paisij were heirs and continuators of the same hesychast tradition.

What did Paisij know of Manjava Skete, its founder, and the way of life there? These questions cannot be answered with any certainty, but Paisij must have had some knowledge of Manjava. In his wanderings as a young man he must have come across monks, if not from Manjava, then at least who knew the Manjava Skete, and later, after he settled in Moldavia, there is also a chance he knew Manjava. The influence of Manjava Skete, in fact, extended to Moldavia; naturally enough, since it was close to the border with Moldavia and there were constant contacts between ukrainian and moldavian monasteries. Jov's Life speaks of moldavian monks coming to him. The Manjava Skete, however, had particular ties with a prominent moldavian monastery, Sucevčtça, founded in 1580 by the Movila family. In 1642 the hospodar of Moldavia, Basil Lupu, invited monks from Manjava to revive this monastery. Sucevčtça was to be reformed to the common life established by the 'venerable fathers Jov and Theodosius' of Manjava, so that in Moldavia too 'a vine might blossom from that vineyard planted by God'. Five years later the hospodar placed the Sucevčtça monastery in permanent dependence on the Manjava, in which it remained until the Manjava Skete itself was suppressed.[45]

---

44. This biography is in Featherstone, 91–155
45. Celevyč, 53; see also the documents of later hospodars confirming this dependence, pp. xc–xcvi.

THE TEXTS

All three works translated here were published in the nineteenth century by the ukrainian historian A. Petruševyč.[46] In preparing my translation I have compared his edition with the seventeenth-century manuscript that Petruševyč used, the only copy of the texts known so far. The manuscript is now in the Stefanyk Library of the Ukrainian Academy of Sciences in Lviv. In Petruševyč's time all three texts formed a single manuscript, but since then they have been rebound as two volumes in a small format: MV-143 (*Testament*) and MV-144 (*Life* and *Rule*). The *Life* and the *Testament* are written by one hand, in careful and easily legible semi-uncials (*polustav*). The *Rule* is written in another hand; it is also easy to read, but is written carelessly, with numerous slips of the pen, and in a few passages some words may have been left out through inadvertence.

The manuscript, obviously, is not an autograph. In Petruševyč's time it was at the Pidhirci monastery in western Ukraine, from where it came to the Stefanyk Library when monastic libraries were confiscated after 1945. As we saw earlier, the Pidhirci monastery, at the very beginning of the formation of its monastic community, adopted the rule and customs of Manjava. Very likely the three works were copied at Manjava expressly at the request of the Pidhirci monastery. Similar copies may have been made for other monasteries that looked to Manjava as their model. Manuscripts that once belonged to ukrainian monasteries have been so little studied that it is quite possible that some other copies may yet be discovered.

In transcribing the manuscripts, Petruševyč, like many editors of his time, to some extent modernized and stan-

---

46. Jov's *Life* as Жизнь преподобнаго отца Iова', *Зоря Галицка яко альбом на год 1860* [*Zorja Halycka jako albom na hod 1860*] (Lviv 1860) 225–251; the *Testament* and the *Rule* in 'Акты относящиеся к истории южно-западной Русн', *Науковый сборник* 4 (1868) 109–155.

dardized the orthography; his edition is also not free from typographical errors. The text itself, however, Petruševyč gives integrally and faithfully, with one exception. Only in one section of Jov's *Life*—here given as '7. Jov is Engaged in Church Affairs'—did Petruševyč intentionally omit a few phrases. Every time the term 'uniate' or ' union' appears in this passage, he replaced it with an ellipsis. These few omissions arose from the particular political circumstances around 1860 in western Ukraine, then within the Austrian empire. Petruševyč's excisions were due to a short-lived attempt to court all political currents in ukrainian society by omitting phrases that referred in disparaging terms to the union of the Ruthenian Church with Rome. Other than these few omissions of one or two words, all in one paragraph, the printed text is exactly that of the manuscript.

The writings are given here in an integral translation. In the manuscript the chief mark of punctuation is a period, placed after every few words, without regard for sentence structure. Petruševyč adopted a modern system of punctuation, but in my translation I often separate sentences differently than did he. The original text also has very few paragraph divisions. Petruševyč added a few others, but I have introduced many more. I have also provided all the subtitles in the *Life*; the subtitles of the *Testament* and the *Rule* are in the manuscript text, marked in red ink.

All the scriptural references have been inserted by me. The Manjava authors quote from Scripture in Church Slavonic, in a translation that derives from the Greek; for the Old Testament, this means the Septuagint version. In not a few cases the text of these citations differs from the Hebrew Old Testament and from New Testament texts that serve as the basis for modern translations. The authors quote scriptural verses from memory, often as these verses are found in church offices; the citations are not always exact, and sometimes several texts are conflated. I have therefore translated all scriptural citations and references directly from the texts. The references to chapter and verse are to greek versions and to translations based on them.

I have provided references to the works or lives of the Fathers cited in the Manjava writings whenever this was possible. The authors also cite the Fathers from memory, sometimes faultily, as I note in one place. Theodosius refers to the *Paterika* and *Gerontika*. Although no clear-cut distinction can be made, by the *Paterika*, roughly speaking, are meant collections of lives or of incidents of lives of the Fathers, usually grouped by region or monastery, in other words, to such works as the History of the Monks in Egypt; while the *Gerontika* are the various collections of the apophthegmata, sayings of the Fathers. In either case, it is no easy matter to trace the particular collection of lives or sayings from which Theodosius' citations are culled.[47]

Other works too present a problem. The output of Saint John Chrysostom is so vast, to say nothing of the numberless spurious works that circulated under his name, that it is a hopeless task to trace a quote without any further indications. Saint Ephrem the Syrian was a favorite of the monks, but his works have been little known in the West and as yet there is no critical edition or modern translation of his penitential sermons and exhortations to monks. The works of Saint Isaac the Syrian present a special problem. The translation of his writings into Greek was more a paraphrase, and this greek version served as the basis for a translation into Slavic. References to Saint Isaac's works can be only

---

47. Partially this is because Slavic MSS of apophthegmata and related collections have been little studied As Jer'omin, in his very limited overview of the MSS, cited in fn. 6 above, points out, there is even a great confusion in assigning the same conventional titles such as the Skete Paterikon, to vastly different collections of apophthegmata and anecdotes. For a Slavic translation of the 'Ανδρῶν αγίων βίβλος, see Nikolaas van Wijk, *The Old Church Slavonic Translation of the* Ανδρῶν αγίων βίβλος' (The Hague: Mouton 1975), from, basically, a fourteenth-century bulgarian manuscript; unfortunately, this posthumous publication, prepared in the 1930s, lacks an index, which greatly diminishes its usefulness.

to the greek and slavic versions or translations made from them, not from the original Syriac.

All works lose something in translation. In the texts from Manjava the echo of liturgical texts is lost. The authors do not explicitly quote from the prayers they were used to reciting, but their language is imbued with words, with phrases, with a way of putting ideas into words that draws on the prayers of the office that frequent repetition had made fully their own. Even if references were possible, they would not serve: a connection between two similar expressions can be observed by anyone, but the significance of the expression can be caught only by one who knows those texts as well, as personally, as did those monks.

The Texts

.

THE LIFE OF JOV OF MANJAVA

THE LIFE OF OUR VENERABLE FATHER JOV,
AND HIS PASSING AWAY,
AND THE ESTABLISHMENT OF
THE HOLY SKETE CENOBIUM,
BRIEFLY DESCRIBED.

Bless, holy father, [the reading]:

INTRODUCTION

T O WRITE AND TO READ the lives of
the saints is useful and praiseworthy,
while to imitate their lives and do
what they did is pious and God-pleasing.
*The just man, when he comes to die, will be
in peace,* says the wisdom of God.† [The just
man] truly says, with the prophet: *Blessed is
the Lord, who will not give us over to be seized by
their teeth. My soul like a bird has been saved from
the catchers' net; the net broke, and I was saved.*†
And: *the just man will be remembered eternally.*†
How true this is, beloved! Indeed, the Holy
Spirit in this way made blessed him who
began in righteousness and died in holiness
and whose life passed from this to that most
peaceful and never-ending world, *where there
is no pain nor sorrow nor sighing, but eternal life,*[1]
in the Father and the Son and the Holy Spirit.

cf.Ws 3: 3

Ps 123: 6–7
Ps 111: 6

---

1. This is a commonly recurring phrase in prayers for the dead in the
byzantine rite.

69

Why should we bury in the sands of silence the memory of our father, our founder and our guide, and his life, his *podvyhy*, his zeal for the pious faith and the dogmas of holy Church, and especially his zeal for the evangelical and apostolic common life. This work will make known also his other virtues, which he gathered into his soul like a precious treasure, in preparation for his end. We intend to describe how and where and what virtues he acquired, so that others too, having seen and read about such godly zeal, may turn it to their own benefit. Above all, may we and those who come after us have it as a stimulus to love *podvyhy* and our monastery and to imitate his zeal.

Truly, a new Job appeared in our times, bearing the same name as the one who lived in the sun-drenched East—and not only his name, but also his virtues. He came not from the Abyssinian land, but from Little Russia, from that part of the Halyč region that is called Pokuttja, from the town Tysmjanycja.[2] That one in the sun-drenched East was of noble birth, immaculate, just, and honest, a worshiper of God, who strove to purify himself from all evil;[†] for the great Job did not lose patience. Our venerable father Jov adorned himself by imitating his life, for not less did he shine forth in the tranquillity of stillness,[3] in his skete by the stream Baters, like Elias at Cherith, and other holy anchorites. He was of

Jb 1:1

---

2. In western Ukraine, in an angle (*kut*) formed by the Prut and Dniester rivers and the Carpathian mountains. For *Little Russia*, see Glossary under *Rus'*.

3. See Glossary under *stillness*.

noble birth, as our account will relate further
on, just and immaculate, not only a true
worshiper of God, but a God-bearer. *I will
come to dwell in them, says the Scripture, and
will walk with them and I will be their God.*† The
former strove to purify himself from all evil;
the latter became wholly a temple of the Holy
Spirit, in utter purity. He was besides a model
of purification for those who came to him
with the desire to be saved. As the Lord says:
*I and the Father will come to him and dwell in
him,*† and this indeed came to be.

2 Cor 6:16

cf. Jn 14:23

On account of this purification of his heart,
two weeks before his soul departed from his
body, when he was already mortally sick, his
lips ceaselessly repeated that hymn of Saint
John Damascene about the Holy Trinity (tone
three): *I glorify the power of the Father and the
Son and sing the praises of the lordship of the Holy
Spirit, indivisible uncreated divinity, Trinity in
one essence, reigning for endless ages.*[4] He could
not have enough of singing this hymn and the
other verses about the divinity of Christ and
his incarnation and sufferings and resurrection. When I was still living with him in the
holy monastery at Uhornyky, I often saw him
during the church offices, when a verse about
the Holy Trinity was being chanted, or when
the *Glory be to the Father and to the Son and to
the Holy Spirit* was read or he himself read it,
a great fear would come upon him, and an
ineffable joy flowed from his inmost being,
transforming his face and gladdening all of
us. His countenance then showed fear at the
overwhelming majesty and might of God, but

---

4. From the byzantine office, Sunday evening vespers.

also joy, on account of his mercy: God shows such condescension to human beings, as to permit them to gaze upon him and to sing his praises together with the heavenly host. Upon whom even the six-winged cherubim and all the heavenly host may not gaze, human beings whose minds have been purified continually contemplate and delight in the sight of his beauty.

As he was himself, so also he taught the brethren to be: 'Know, my fathers and brothers, that we are called orthodox, because in our doxology in church and in solitude the holy life-giving and indivisible Trinity is always glorified. For that reason, when the doxology comes in the singing and in the psalms, the praises of the one Godhead in three Persons are to be chanted with great fear and sobriety. The Scripture says: *I will glorify those who in fear glorify me.*[†] Those who in temerity and without feeling stand before him and sing his praises the Lord will cast away and destroy.'

It is terrible to fall into the hands of the living God, for our God is a devouring fire.[†] For that reason, fathers and brethren, God has greatly glorified him. He was found worthy to be honored with the splendor that God has prepared for those who love him, which eye has not seen nor ear heard nor has it entered the heart of a man immersed in passions.[†] He has entered into the joy of his Lord, because he doubled the talent entrusted to him,[†] for he was all things to all men, according to the Apostle.[†] When the parched, enflamed by heretical allurements or carnal lusts or the vanities of this world came to

Cf. Ps 14:4; 1 Sm 2:30

Heb 10:31; 12:29

Cf. 1 Cor 2:9

Cf. Mt 25: 14–23
1 Cor 9:22

him, after drinking of the grace of his teaching their burning thirst would be slaked and they would depart glorifying God, who has given such a man in these latter times. Similarly, when someone blinded by a host of passionate desires came, he would be enlightened by his teaching as by a lamp shining in the sight of all.† Cf. Mt 5:16

Many, then, desired to imitate his godly life and his *podvyh*, hence they would not go back, but would choose to suffer poverty and his other *podvyhy*, for the sake of the heavenly kingdom, or, rather, for the sake of the love of God, which they saw shining in him, after which to return to the world was like returning to the darkness of Egypt.

Let us begin at the beginning, however: where his godly life began and how he was granted such grace. *A tree is recognized by its fruit.*† It is right that we should find out Mt 12:33 about his home and his parents, since this is of no small benefit to those who seek what is useful. As for those who take scandal, let them take scandal, for woe to those who call light darkness.† We, then, will begin at the Cf. Is 5:20 beginning and narrate his life.

EARLY YEARS

Our venerable father, as we mentioned above, was born in Tysmjanycja of noble parents with the family name Knjahynyc'kyj; they were quite well off.[5] He was raised in the

---

5. On the basis of the dates and Jov's age that Ignatius gives further on in the *Life*, we can place Jov's birth around 1550.

knowledge and fear of God and was given instruction in reading and writing; he liked books and learned quickly. As was proper, he was obedient to his parents. Under the inspiration of God his parents then sent him to the holy monastery Univ for further schooling. There he assiduously and with docility studied all he was taught, and also the prayers of the office. He listened attentively to the reading of the divine scriptures and came to know the order of monastic life, so that everyone marveled.

After this, he went on to the God-protected town Ostrih, to finish his studies. At that time this was ruled by the pious prince Basil with his sons.[6] The youth entered the school there and studied assiduously; soon he was to be, instead of a student, a teacher of others. He was always meek, given to silence, and charitable to the poor, gracious towards his companions; he always conducted himself in the fear of God. The pious prince and his children got to know him well; he even copied out the Psalter for the young prince Alexander, since he was a gifted copyist of the divine scriptures.

A TRIP TO MOUNT ATHOS

At that time a certain hieromonk Varlaam from the Holy Mountain happened to come

6. Ostroh was the family seat of the Ostroz'kyj princes and the center of their extensive properties. The prince Basil referred to here is better known under his other name Constantine (c.1526–1608), a man of great wealth and influence. He founded a famous school at Ostrih, with Ruthenian and Greek scholars as teachers, among them Cyril, the later patriarch of Constantinople, who is mentioned further on in this *Life* (below, note 38).

to the pious prince Basil for alms, with a letter from the holy fathers living there. When the pious prince Basil read it, he at once began to consider whom he could send with them, someone faithful and prudent, so that the alms would reach them whole and entire and he would not be shamed before the fathers there.

After thinking this over for a long time, he decided to send Ioan (this was Jov's name originally), since he saw that Ioan was more skillful in such affairs than other persons. For some time Ioan had been faithfully serving prince Basil's principal retainer, Lord Peter, the *starosta* of Smidyn'. The prince, then, entrusted what he was sending to Ioan.

With God's help and by the prayers of the holy fathers they soon reached the Holy Mountain; there the holy fathers received them with great love and benevolence and saw to it that they had all they needed during their stay. Ioan went around the holy monasteries, as the prince's servant and an honored guest. In all the monasteries the fathers received him with honor and showed him their customs. He, on his part, wept at the miserable emptiness of the life of this world and reflected that there is nothing useful in it, but only the lust of the flesh and the concupiscence of the eyes, as the Apostle says.[†] He saw the common life like a second paradise and the monks like other immaterial angels. He saw the befitting beauty of the churches and their services, like a second heaven, and he saw the solitudes surrounded by orchards; above all, he saw no one of the female sex, not even animals, unless a wild one or a bird

1 Jn 2:16

flying through the air. Soon he forgot himself, ruing the years he had already lived, since he considered them to have been lived in vain, and only because of urgent duty he went back, to render the thanks of the holy fathers and to report how he had acquitted himself when he brought them the alms.

Protected by God's grace and the prayers of the holy fathers, he returned to the pious prince, bearing him greetings from the Holy Mountain and from those who live there and acquitted himself of the task entrusted to him with a very satisfactory account; he also asked to be discharged. The prince thanked him greatly for his service and rewarded him, then dismissed him in peace. Once he was free of his charge, Ioan, assisted by God's grace, turned at once to his resolve, recalling the promise he had made to those holy fathers when he was leaving the Holy Mountain, especially to the spiritual father to whom he had committed his conscience, of returning to live with them. He immediately began to sever his ties with the world, since a marriage was being urged upon him, together with the promise of great wealth. That devout soul, however, counted all this as rubbish[†] and, enflamed with Christ's love, he spent even all that he owned on alms, leaving nothing for himself, not even what he might need for the long journey on foot.

Cf. Phil 3:8

As a Monk on Mount Athos

After he had freed his mind completely from all turmoil, he again started out, with some others, for the Holy Mountain, to return as he had promised, carrying not an olive branch, like the dove returning to him who had let him out of the ark,† but bringing himself as a living sacrifice to the Lord Christ. As Abraham willed to offer Isaac, so he willed to give over his body into service, that the flesh might be in bondage to the spirit. When with God's help he reached the places that he longed for, he went around all the holy monasteries with joy, visiting them and praying in them; he desired to imitate the elders in their solitary cells and in the sketes and in the caves, and asked their prayers.

Cf. Gn 8: 9

He next gave himself over to obedience to a certain elder, hieromonk Isidore, who was living in a skete, about whose life everyone testified that he was a man of great *podvyh*; indeed, he was a wonderworker after death. Ioan submitted to him in all things and took pains to carry out everything enjoined on him with faith, inscribing in his heart all the godly corrections of his elder. He remained in this *podvyh* under that blessed elder a year and a half, then the elder tonsured him to the *rjasa*. Seeing him young and strong of body, the elder then said to him: 'Since you are young, you need to serve in the cenobitic life,' and gave him over to the holy monastery called Vatopedi.[7] The fathers there embraced him, as is the custom, and counted him as one of their community; they assigned to him the obedience of *magopia*,[8] that is, breadbaking.

7. Cenobitic life was introduced at the Vatopedi monastery on Athos in 1575 and lasted for some years, when the idiorrhythmic way of life again took hold. Jov's years at Vatopedi fall within this brief cenobitic interlude.

8. More correctly, *mankipion*.

Ioan served in this with all meekness and the
fear of God, humbly submitting to all those
who were older, working not as for men, but
as for Christ himself. They then deemed him
worthy of the angelic habit, and his name was
changed to Ezechiel.

Then, after some years, seeing his desire
for stillness, they gave him a small tower
for his cell, to live there in tranquillity, since
his guileless obedience was evident to all.
He was truly industrious, and his repose
was to work with his hands—his manual
work was bookbinding. He came to know
the Greek language thoroughly and also the
church order; he was of keen intelligence
and had an excellent memory. He remained
there, in the obedience of the common life
for twelve years, without ever going away.
It then happened that they were sending out
some monks to collect alms, and after much
deliberation they decided to send also our
father Ezechiel, together with several elders,
to Great Russia, since they knew that he was
skillful and of help in all things and that
he had a good command of both the Greek
and the Ruthenian language. They dismissed
them in peace.

When they returned from the task given
them with abundant alms, Ezechiel again
desired to live the solitary life in a skete.
He gathered many virtues from many *podvyžnyky*, like an industrious bee, so that in him
could be seen David's meekness, wisdom
like Solomon's, Moses' gentleness, chastity
like Joseph's, discernment like Daniel's, zeal
for the faith and for the monastic life like

Ezechiel's, absence of acquisitiveness and love of solitude, a pure body, perseverance in fasting like the great John the Baptist's, love like Paul's.[9] Do you see how many good things he obtained through his humility?

With the blessing of the fathers then, he settled in a cave, wearing out his body with hunger, thirst, all-night standing in prayer, compunction, and tears, discarding the old man with his works and putting on the new,[†] *Cf. Eph 4:22–24* created in the image of God,[†] and fulfilling *Cf. Gn 1:26* in act those words of the Apostle: *the world is crucified to me, and I to the world;*[†] as also, *Gal 6:14* *It is no longer I that live, but Christ lives in me.*[†] He chose moderation in all things, a *Gal 2:20* high degree of abstemiousness in food and drink and sleep, constant compunction with sorrow and contriteness of heart before the Lord, Christ God. During the offices in church he stood with great fear and awe, remaining motionless, with bowed head. It can truly be said that he imitated the ancient holy fathers in all things. The holy fathers who lived on the Holy Mountain marveled greatly at the *podvyh* of this man and glorified God for it.

It happened then that the fathers again sent to Rus'[10] their superior Pachomius for alms, and with him a few elders, among them also our father Ezechiel—although he did not want to go—since he knew well that country and language. Rather, this was God's doing, so that he would return to Rus', to his own

---

9. These comparisons are traditional in hymns of the byzantine office on the feasts of fathers and monks, as for Saint Basil (1 January), Saint Antony the Great (17 January), and others.

10. See Glossary.

country, to enlighten it and to plant good
observances there.

RETURN TO UKRAINE

When they came to Little Russia they heard of
great disorders in Moscow and they could not
go on.[11] They waited, therefore, all summer,
using up the provisions they had brought
with them; they then returned to Moldavia, to
their *metochion*, but our father Ezechiel, with
their blessing, remained here. God wanted
this for the benefit of us who live here. So
he stayed, living as a pilgrim for some time
in a house belonging to one of his relatives in
the small town Tysmjanycja.

The noble Balabans, father Gedeon, bishop
of Halyč [and Lviv],[†] and father Isaias, archimandrite of Univ, heard about him and begged him to come to the holy monastery of
Univ, to show them the proper order of
cenobitic life according to the custom of the
Holy Mountain. He did not dare refuse, but
humbly obeyed, for the sake of Christ's commandment and the evangelical common life.
When he came there he did and taught,[†] establishing good order in church and in the
refectory, himself being an example to all by
his continence, vigils, prayers. With the help
of God's grace, he accomplished what he set
out to do, and so began to think about going

bishop 1569–
1607

Cf. Acts 1:1

---

11. The Rjurikide dynasty of Moscow became extinct with the death
of tsar Theodore in January 1598. This was the beginning of the so-called
Period of Troubles, marked by disorders and wars, which lasted until
1618.

back to the Holy Mountain, where he had been tonsured. He knew well that if someone ends his life in the same monastery where he was tonsured, even if he had not observed unusually great *podvyhy*, but only lived in humility and patience, in despoiling his own will and in obedience with faith to the superior, such a monk will unfailingly be crowned with the crown [of victory] by the Judge on the terrible day of his coming. God, however, wanted to retain him here, and so, in his mercy, visited an illness upon him, since, being all-seeing, God knew that on account of him many would evade the enemy's net, to follow him in the monastic life.

In this sickness he became deaf and he assumed the great angelic habit, that is, the schema. It was a wonder to see in a material body an immaterial man, or rather, an angel. Here is an example. In his sickness he happened to glance at his knife, hanging in its sheath, and he grew ashamed. He became displeased and angry with himself, and said, 'How are you going to lead the common life if you have your own knife? Woe is me, how am I going to be, where am I going? Grant me health, Master, that I may repent and have time to serve you in piety and truth.' He cast the knife away and said, 'May this not be counted as sin against me, I beg you, my Lord, Jesus Christ'.

What a marvel, beloved. Truly, fathers and brothers, he appeared greater than those fathers of old, because they had many teachers, some even had angels instructing them, while in these latter times goodness has decreased,

Pss 13:11; 53:3;
cf. Rom 3:12

as the prophet says: *there is no one who does good, no, not one,*[†] because all seek their own and not their neighbor's benefit, from the oldest to the youngest they are enmeshed in love of money and pleasures and vanity. Many lay claim to noble birth, not being such, eager to seize some glory and to be adorned with the finery of this world, abandoning the glory that is from God alone, the freedom and beauty of the heavenly kingdom, the possession of all the saints, who renounced the world and lived patiently in meekness and poverty.

But our father was not like this. He hastened not only to put aside the noble title of this world, which fallen nature considers as the freedom of this world, but cut off even attachment to a knife, in order to submit himself only to Christ and to become adorned with the light of his kingdom. When he recovered from his illness, he again undertook a life of extreme severity, and he insisted on the order of common life, but not everyone listened to his exhortations.

Bishop Gedeon wanted to confer priestly ordination on him, but he would by no means consent to this. Because of the lack of submission among the brethren he grew tired of life at Univ and wanted to go away, since he desired stillness, to which he had become accustomed on the Holy Mountain.

THE FOUNDING OF UHORNYKY MONASTERY

At that point Lord Adam Balaban made a request of him. 'If you want to live in stillness,' he said, 'then on my properties there is a little church of the holy leader of the angelic hosts Michael. I will provide everything that is needed, only you live there as a monk and pray to God for us.[12] If you should want to accept brethren who are of the same mind, I, together with my wife, will give you what is necessary, because I would like to have on my property persons of prayer and a monastery.'

When the elder Jov (the name he took when he assumed the schema) heard this, he thanked him very much for what he promised. He came at once to Uhornyky, to the church of the holy archangel Michael and began to live as a solitary. After a short time many people began to come to him, as to a lamp on a lampstand, both monks and laymen who wanted to live with him and save their souls, seeing him persevering in fasting, in vigils, in uninterrupted prayer. He, like a father who loves his children, accepted those who begged him and who promised to bear hardships patiently and obediently with him. Others he would instruct and teach, then send back.

Soon the fame of his common way of life spread through all Rus'. At that time Isaac of the Holy Mountain, who later was ordained bishop by the patriarch of Jerusalem, received from prince Basil [Ostroz'kyj] the Derman' monastery under his charge.[13] This Isaac begged our father to come to him in

12. 'Live as a monk' here is *spasajsja*, which means literally 'to work out one's salvation'; see the Introduction. Cf. just below, the passage about those who wanted to live with Jov and 'save their souls'.

13. Derman', not far from Ostrih, belonged to Ostroz'kyj, who at this time was engaged in reviving monastic life in the Holy Cross monastery,

order to establish common life there. Jov could not refuse, but with the counsel of his brethren he left one of them as *dikei* in his place and, after instructing them, went to Derman'. His stay there was of benefit to many. He assisted in spiritual as well as in corporal works, even in the typography: an Octoechos was being printed just then.[14]

After that he returned to his monastery at Uhornyky. At that time his friend, Father Ioan Vyšens'kyj, came from the Holy Mountain and stayed with him for some time.[15] Afterwards the two took counsel of each other, and our elder, who wanted to lead an extremely strict life of stillness, committed the superiorship to his disciple, the hierodeacon Herasym, and went off to a solitude some four distances away; he took with him only a little bread and a small book, as did the great Antony, and Apollo, and other venerable fathers.[16]

---

just then (c. 1602) coming out of a period of decline. Isaac Boryskovyč had been a monk on Athos; in 1620 he was ordained Orthodox bishop of Luc'k by patriarch Theophanes III of Jerusalem, who at that time was traveling through Ruthenian lands.

14. An *Octoechos*, one of the books used in the byzantine office, contains the daily services for each of the eight chant tones; the Derman' edition, the first *Octoechos* printed in Ukraine, was begun in 1602 and came out in 1604. Jov, who knew Greek well, would have been invaluable in helping to establish a correct text by checking the slavic translation against the Greek.

15. Ioan Vyšens'kyj (c. 1550–after 1620), noted ukrainian athonite monk and polemicist against the Latin Church and against western learning and influences.

16. The distance given in the text is four *popryšča*, a term used to indicate several widely different measures of distance. Here it probably means the distance of one day's journey, hence Jov traveled four days away from Uhornyky. For the example of Antony the Great, see the *Life of Antony* by

THE FOUNDING OF MANJAVA SKETE

It so happened that he met and became acquainted with Lord Peter Ljaxovyč, who at that time was *župnyk* and held the *ban* from the *starosta* of Halyč.[17] Jov inquired of him about the mountains and deserted places in that region, where he might find a place suitable for a life of stillness in a skete. That Christ-loving man himself readily went with the elder, taking with him men who knew places appropriate for that purpose. After going through a mountain pass up the river called Maneva, which name others give to a hill there by the stream Baters, he found it greatly to his liking. On the hill that God-loving man possessed a small field. Jov at once constructed himself a shelter of plaited wattles[18] under a fir tree, like a second Elias, and began to live alone a very strict life, doing violence to his nature by hunger, thirst, vigils, work, shedding the old man with his deeds and putting on the new.†   Eph 4:22–24

That Christ-loving Peter from the *ban* visited him often, bringing him what he needed, and built him a little cell. Jov rejoiced, because he had obtained the stillness he desired.

Saint Athanasius of Alexandria (NPNF, 2nd series, 4 [rpt Grand Rapids: Eerdmans 1979] 188–221); for Apollo, see Russell.

17. *Župnyk* and *ban* are serbian terms (the second also wallachian), here used to indicate an administrator of a region, dependent on the Halyč *starosta*.

18. The phrase *constructed himself a shelter,* is the same as that used in the Slavic Bible to designate the Jewish feast of Tabernacles (Jn 7:2; cf. Lv 2:33–44). This, like the frequent references to the Gospels and the writings of the Apostles, serves to underline the scriptural foundation for Jov's way of life.

Ceaselessly he sang the praises of his Master,
with the thought of his departure from the
body and of Christ's second coming and
how it would be to stand before his dread
judgment-seat and give an answer for his
deeds and acts and thoughts. Ceaselessly his
tears flowed, as he thought of the good things
prepared for those engaged in *podvyh* and of
the shame and eternal torment for the lazy
like himself and for sinners. Thus he lived as
a solitary, communing only with fear.[19]

The brothers whom he had left at the
monastery of the holy leader of the heavenly
hosts Michael, whom he had not told that
he intended to go away, heard about him
and began to visit him. He would lovingly
instruct them and beg them to keep to the
common life as they had begun when he was
with them and had given their promises in
writing.

A certain meek elder, by the name of
Athanasius, came then to him from that monastery and begged him to let him live the skete
life together with him; Jov received him, and
he lived there to his death. Afterwards Ioan
Vyšens'kyj came with the boy Dmytro, Jov's
nephew, whom the elder had committed to
his charge, and he too stayed quite a long
time, since he too greatly loved silence and
was a holy and hard-working man, as many
people can witness. Thus there were four of
them living in full concord.[20]

19. Fear of God, of course, the beginning of wisdom, cf. Ps 110:10, and
others.
20. Literally, *living as if having one soul,* one of the many allusions to
Acts 4:32.

A certain clairvoyant said to our elder: 'Elder Jov,' he said, 'your labors here will not be in vain, because here many will follow your way of life, serving God in piety and truth, and a great monastery will arise here for the glory of Christ God. Even if you go away, and I too, this place will not remain deserted, but monks will live here.' The elder said: 'May the Lord's will be done'. Interiorly he prayed continuously: *Not to us, but to your name be glory.*[†] I beg you, my Master and Creator, raise again among our people the evangelical Christian life that has waned, a monasticism lived with *podvyh* and common life according to your commandments, for the renewal and adornment of your holy Church, as it was formerly in Rus', at the time of our holy fathers Antony and Theodosius and the others who shone forth in the cave in the town of Kiev.[21] With the passing of time and a change of persons, piety has waned and the good order of monastic common life has been extinguished, and monasteries have become deserted. Raise again by your divine grace the fervor of your people and give us zeal and love for the *podvyhy* and life of our fathers, since we have greatly degenerated. Help us, o God our Savior, that we not perish and the heathen say: where is their God.'[†] This prayer he often had in his heart and many times also repeated it out loud.

Ps 113: 9

Cf. Jl 2:17

Ioan Vyšens'kyj, after having lived some time here, again went off to the Holy Mountain, leaving the boy with Jov. He advised

---

21. The reference is to the founders of monasticism in Ukraine, see the Introduction.

and begged the elder not to depart from
these mountains and solitude, because this,
he said, was a fitting place for those who
seek salvation.[22] So indeed it turned out as
he said, because after his departure monks
and laymen who wanted to imitate Jov's life
began to come and wanted to stay with him.
Jov would teach them what was useful and
admonish them to fear God and to strive to
carry out his commandments and to preserve
purity of soul and body, above all, to keep
the orthodox faith unaltered to the end, and
would dismiss them. Others he would send
to the cenobitic life at Uhornyky. He would
accept very few to stay with him, so that
his rule of stillness might not be impaired.
Even though he accepted some, these, after
living there a little, could not endure his strict
asceticism and departed.

JOV IS ENGAGED IN CHURCH AFFAIRS

At that time Gedeon Balaban, exarch of the
great see of Constantinople and bishop of
Lviv, passed away.[23] Then the blessed elder,

---

22. A letter from Ioan Vyšens'kyj to Jov survives, written some years
later, when Jov was already living in solitude at the place called Mark's,
AJuZR, 7 (Kiev 1887) 36–37.

23. Bishop Gedeon Balaban died on 10 February 1607. His title of
exarch signified that he represented the patriarch of Constantinople in
Ukraine and had jurisdiction over stauropegial institutions. The following
passage deals with the succession to the Lviv see, which both Uniates
and Orthodox wanted to secure for their candidate. As it turned out,
the Lviv eparchy remained Orthodox until 1700, when its bishop, Joseph
Šumljans'kyj, accepted union with Rome. Gedeon's successor in the see
was Jeremias Tysarovs'kyj, 1607–1641.

like a good sentinel and defender of piety, was greatly distressed. With all his might he strove to preserve this eparchy from the deceitful heretical uniate incursion (this is the only eparchy to remain free up until now), with prayer to God and fasting, also with vigils, to which he also urged the brethren. He also labored much, traveling on foot, persuading and begging townsmen, eminent priests, and well-born nobles to stand courageously by the holy apostolic Church and her dogmas and to strive to elect a worthy man to that bishopric, and to be on the watch against and avoid with loathing any uniate seduction. On account of this he was much humiliated, scorned, and derided by people who considered themselves true orthodox; he bore this with all meekness, for the Lord's sake, in imitation of other saints who suffered for piety's sake. When he saw that nothing was successful and how few were those who zealously clung to piety, while the rest were like reeds shaken by the wind, who elected a bishop without having a right to this, he, enflamed by the love of God, hastened to Moldavia. He journeyed to the metropolitan [of Iasçi], so that he would not ordain the bishop-elect until the latter swore an oath before many witnesses and before the holy and life-giving cross and on the holy Gospels, under pain of the anathema of the 318 holy fathers[†] and of the other holy councils, that he would not be swayed by the allurements and false good of the union with Rome; also, that he would guard firmly and undauntedly to the end of his life the see entrusted to

The first ecumenical council of Nicea

him. Jov did not desist until he had obtained this.

He wanted himself to receive this oath. He faced the bishop—elect and with great zeal according to God begged him with tears not to subject that holy see to the union: 'watch out that you may not inherit, in place of the Apostles' portion, that of Judas.' The bishop was greatly amazed at his zeal, because Jov never acted out of human respect, but spoke out to all with deep feeling about the teachings of the Orthodox faith. 'I,' said the bishop, 'will not hesitate to shed my blood even for the least point of the Orthodox holy catholic eastern Church.' The Lord did not despise his labors and zeal and has preserved that eparchy to this day unharmed and whole from being carried away by the enticements of the uniates.

Life in Manjava Skete

Jov returned to his community and resumed his previous life of stillness. Many brethren were coming who wanted to live with him and begged him to accept them. Among them was a certain Proxor, who lived for a long time in *podvyh* and meekness in this holy monastery, who carried out every kind of service until his death. The elder would admit those who promised to remain until death after they had pleaded much and stood a long trial. He accepted them as members, to be like one body and soul, having one heart and mind.†

Cf. Acts 4:32

He honored and loved everyone as himself,

according to the Lord's commandment, and
he consoled all as his friends, out of the living
love, which is God, that was in him.

He also taught the brethren to bear the
mark of Christ's disciples: *By this all will
recognize that you are my disciples, if you have
true love among yourselves.*† He himself did
nothing without first proposing it to those
who lived with him and seeking their advice,
all of them being of one mind. He did this
not because he did not know what to do, but
out of respect for his neighbor and because,
as he said, such is the order of common life
and this is what it means to be of one mind,
according to Saint Basil.²⁴ He had such a
high regard for the community of love that
nothing was put out to eat or to drink in
the refectory unless there was enough for
everyone; if it did not suffice for everyone,
he would absolutely forbid it to be served.
He said that he preferred to have it spoil or to
give it to other persons rather than to destroy
the common order of piety for the sake of a
small morsel.

Their occupation was to sing continually
the praises of God, with a pure heart and conscience, without slackening. He established
the canonical hours according to the practice of the Holy Mountain, that is, the morning office with chanting in common and the
prayer rule in private. There was then time
for reading and for manual work, also for
assigned tasks; then, after the ninth hour was

Jn 13:35

24. Again, a reference to Acts 4:32. In Basil references to being of one
mind and to the common life are frequent, but see especially his *Regulae
fusius tractatae* (Long Rules) 7 (Clarke, 163; Wagner, 247).

read, the meal was at a fixed time. It is worth mentioning the meals in the refectory. When he lived alone, Jov followed a very severe regimen on bread and water, and even this only after the ninth hour, often every other day or every two days. When he accepted brethren to live with him, however, he permitted cooking without oil, of whatever there was by turns, but with moderation. Drink was water or vegetable broth.

They would work physically one or two hours: now to prepare wood for their needs, now to strip the inner bark off the logs. The bark would be brought to the monks and the brethren would sew small baskets from it, sometimes Jov himself would be busied with the sewing. The brethren made spoons and crosses from cedar wood and did other handwork. This they gave to pious persons who visited them and brought them alms.

Sometimes in the autumn they would go through the wilderness gathering the mushrooms that are called *ryžky*; these they would salt and in the wintertime would have them for food for themselves and for any visitors who might come. When the elder sent his brethren to solitary places to gather these mushrooms or other things, he would appoint one of them to be in charge and would recommend that their excursion be orderly, with the fear of God and with submission. They were to preserve brotherly love among themselves and unceasingly have the Jesus prayer interiorly, reciting: *Lord Jesus Christ, Son of God, have mercy on me, a sinner.* He used to say that whoever does not have this prayer continuously and purely in his heart has no arms for combat. He himself throughout his life always kept this prayer, his lips unceasingly moving in repeating it.

Saturdays and Sundays there were two meals, when, by God's favor, someone of the faithful would bring him oil or fish, especially the lord Peter Ljaxovyč mentioned above. He received such presents as from the hands of Christ. They would partake of such gifts only on Saturdays and Sundays.[25] They never touched butter or cheese, whether made from cow-milk or sheep-milk. This order and tradition with regard to the office and the refectory and work his disciples observe in his monastery to the present day.

THE FIRST VISIT OF THEODOSIUS

So he lived according to the divine Apostle, forgetting what was past and stretching out to what was before,[†] with all sobriety. He ceaselessly prayed to Christ to send them someone who might have the grace from on high of being ordained by the imposition of a bishop's hands, that is, a priest.

Cf. Phil 3:13

At that time the hierodeacon Theodosius came, who had been tonsured and ordained in Moldavia, in the monastery of the immaculate Mother of God called Putna. The elder was overjoyed to see him and loved him greatly, since he had known him still

---

25. Saturday is not a fast day in the byzantine tradition, although in the four fast seasons (see *Testament*, ch.12), the fast is not broken either on Saturday or on Sunday.

as a secular. He affectionately greeted him
and asked him everything about where he
had been, and where and by whom he had
been tonsured, and how and why he left
that place, and why he came here. The deacon recounted everything exactly, in a god-
fearing manner. 'I came, venerable father, for
the sake of spiritual profit and I would like to
be the least of those under the obedience of
your reverence, holy father.' The elder, who
wanted to try him, answered: 'No, my dear
deacon, you can't live here. I live here very
plainly, as is proper in a skete, with two or
three others. But you are a deacon. You have
to live where there is a church, in common
life together with numerous brethren, and to
serve the altar according to your degree [of
ordination]. We don't have a church, since
anchorites don't seek out churches, but to
purify and save their souls in silence and
weeping.' He said this not to reject him, but as
if to rouse his desire to greater love towards
him, because by God's grace he foresaw that
Theodosius was to join them, and through
him God would order the monastery, as indeed happened later. Finally he said, to explain that he was not rejecting him : 'If God
will want us to have a little church in this
solitude, then we may yet be joined in love
in a brotherhood of the common life, if your
desire is not extinguished. For now, go to live
in the monastery at Pitryči, in common life,
in your fatherland, in patience and meekness,
in love of God and love of the brethren.'
(With them had come the *ihumen* of Pitryči,
the hieromonk Father Pankratij.) Jov gave all

of them useful instructions for their life and
dismissed them in peace.

The deacon went away, saddened and joyful: saddened because he had not obtained
what he desired, joyful about the profit and
grace of Jov's words, but especially because
he had confidence in his promise. He stayed
there with them a year and a half, as *econome*.
In his heart, however, the desire to be with
the elder in the solitude grew all the time.

He often visited the elder, to bring him
alms; on such occasions he would confess his
thoughts and go away with great profit for
his soul. Similarly, many monks from other
monasteries would visit him, some to tell him
their thoughts and ask his counsel, others
for the sake of his prayer, still others with
the desire to live with him. He would not
admit them, however, but only instructed
them and urged them to live the common life
where they were tonsured, according to their
promises of obedience to their fathers. To
many, however, he gave in and let them stay
with him for a while for their benefit. Some
notable persons, such as father Isaias Balaban himself, the archimandrite, and father
Zacharias Kopystens'kyj,[26] stayed for quite
some time, in great humility, deriving consolation from his deeds and words, likewise father Petronij Vojutyns'kyj, who stayed a year
and a half, and Kopet and Rudnyc'kyj and
others. They stayed for a longer or shorter
time and, having been consoled, departed.

---

26. A learned ukrainian monk and writer, from 1624 to his death in
1627 archimandrite of the Kiev Lavra.

Similarly, many pious Christians, burghers, nobles, and priests, visited him and had the joy of the consolation that his lips imparted; they would return home greatly praising God. So also Lord Peter Ljaxovyč often visited him, bringing him what was needed.

One time he said: 'Bless [me], elder: I will build you here a small church, for the sake of the many people who come to visit you and the brothers who want to live with you. Don't send them away; I'll take care of all your needs and will supply whatever is necessary for the church.' Upon hearing this, Jov thanked him. 'But,' he said, 'I ask you, beloved of Christ, don't be sparing of your goods in building during your administration first a small church, where you will be commemorated, at the spot called Mark's, for the glory of Christ God and the holy precursor John. Many pious persons come to us and salt merchants pass that way;[27] they would come to a church there, and some of us also go there. As for us, if it is God's will and he gives us his help, there will be time afterwards, if we are alive.' Ljaxovyč received this suggestion with joy, as if it had come from one of God's angels. He lost no time in building a church and outfitting it with icons and books and having it blessed.

Observe the father's discernment and how he kept the evangelical commandments: to love God with all one's soul, since his love desired that the holy name of God be praised

---

27. The region in which Manjava is located has many salt deposits, exploited commercially since prehistoric times.

in all places; and to love one's neighbor as oneself. Actually, he loved his neighbor even more than himself, because unmindful of himself and his own needs he was concerned about what was useful for his neighbor and about his salvation. For this reason God made his name known throughout all Rus', according to his promise: *Those who glorify me, them I will glorify.*†

1 Sm 2:30

A RELOCATION

Jov was greatly embarrassed at being praised by many people and again began to think about returning to the Holy Mountain, where he was tonsured; he gave himself up to prayer and fasting and great sorrow. The brethren who were with him, upon seeing him so downcast and afflicted, were astonished, but did not dare ask him and only wondered among themselves what could have come up so unexpectedly. Perhaps, they thought, he has foreseen his own death, or perhaps some grave trial has come upon him. Jov saw that they were troubled but afraid to ask, so once he said to them: 'Dear brothers and children, I see that you are troubled on account of me, a sinner. I beg you not to be troubled. May God comfort you and teach you as is his will, how to save your souls. I intend to leave you, to return to the Holy Mountain, that my bones may rest in the monastery where I made my vows, as soon as spring comes.'

After giving them many useful instructions about patience and brotherly love, Jov went off to his solitude to spend the night there, as he was often in the habit of doing. There he prayed to God with tears day and night that he might finish his life according to God's will, and he remained without food a day or two. The brethren did not know what he was doing. He made himself a shelter under a tree in which to spend the night, since it was winter.

One day he returned from his solitude with a shining face and a joyful look, totally transformed. The brethren were grieving at his departure, but he, after the reading and the meal, told them: 'My dear brethren, I have thought to move to a solitude further away from the path, near to the stream, to a spot of no use and inaccessible to men and to cattle. Our present location is useful for haying and for cattle grazing, and so that no one may feel hostility towards us, I have found an inaccessible spot (where the monastery is now built) under the hill beyond the streams, like an island.' The brethren were surprised at his words and how suddenly he had changed his mind about going off to the Holy Mountain. Their hearts were lighter as they thanked him. He said to them: 'We can build there our cell and put up a small church'. With warm affection he gave them permission to move the cell that was already standing and to build a church. By God's grace he had received some illumination to build a church and a monastery, in place of Vatopedi of the Holy Mountain a new Vatopedi in Rus', for the bringing up of children according to the spirit and according to the life of the evan-

gelical commandments, as indeed it turned
out. Vatopedi, in fact, in Greek means the
education of youth.[28] There he intended to
establish the rules and customs that he had
observed on the Holy Mountain.

He had the custom of never beginning
anything without first testing it by prayer
and fasting for some time, with patience and
trust in God. After prayer and after taking
counsel with those of one mind, therefore,
he took the brethren and went to the spot
he had found and there he prayed to God
that their undertaking might be according to
his will, and their life be to his glory and to
the benefit of orthodox Christians. He began
to clear off a place for the cell, then told
the brethren to continue clearing it, while he
himself went to a certain Christ-loving lady,
Anastasia Balaban, wife of Voljanovs'kyj. He
told her about his proposal and what he had
started and asked her to build a cell. She
gladly straightway sent skilled workers to
build a spacious cell. Thus he moved to the
new cell, further off in the solitude, in 1611.

THEODOSIUS JOINS THE
COMMUNITY AT MANJAVA

At that time the deacon Theodosius that we
mentioned earlier heard from some people
about that foundation and the elder's intention to move further into the solitude and

28. This is derived from folk etymology, which in Greek confused the
ending *pedi* with *paidia*, education. The true etymology of Vatopedi is
uncertain.

to build there a church and a monastery for the brethren. He felt unhappy in the monastery where he was because of certain conflicts there, since he greatly desired the stillness of solitude. So he left everything and with the blessing of his superior hurried away to the blessed elder. When the elder saw him, he did not dissuade him as before, but encouraged and seconded his desire, not extinguishing his fervor. He received Theodosius with love and admitted him to their life in common. He showed Theodosius the place and what had been begun and told him about his intention to build a church. 'With God's help,' he said, 'there will be a small church here. You, being a deacon, will help us in everything; in fact, it's right that you should be here, since you are from the environs of Halyč, and this place belongs to the *starosta* of Halyč. The *ktytor* likewise is from the Halyč region, so this will be a Halyč monastery, like Pitryči, only be patient and single-minded.' The deacon was all aglow with fervor and love at such an unexpected disposition; he bowed to the ground before Jov and all the brethren and submitted himself to Jov and obeyed him like Christ himself.

A CHURCH IS BUILT

Theodosius, then, began to work with them at clearing the location; they worked hard at digging up tree roots and burning them, moving large logs and supplies from one place to another, and filling up low spots. The terrain was unsuitable in every way: it was uneven, in the shadow of a mountain, with thick woods all around. The elder toiled with great effort with the brethren day and night, not sparing himself, like a voluntary martyr. Then, when the place for the building of a church was more or less cleared, he recalled to the *ktytor* mentioned above, the Lord Peter, his promise. 'Now is the time,' he said, 'if you still have the desire, to build a small church to the glory of Christ our God on that new spot.' The *ktytor* was very happy to hear these words of the elder and himself came with the elder and with his father Vlax (may he rest in peace; he happened just then to be at Mark's place) to inspect that place. When they saw it, they gladly agreed to it. Vlax urged his son Peter to carry it out and to heed the elder in everything and to provide for all the elder's needs as regards the building. He at once sent skilled workmen to prepare the wood, and they began sawing it.

Winter was near, so the elder laid the matter aside. He ordered the wood and the other materials to be stacked together and put off the building until spring. He left hierodeacon Theodosius and the brethren to spend the winter in the cells at the old place and charged Theodosius with the task of beginning the prayer rule and reciting the prayer. The elder indeed always held those in orders in honor. When a priest, be he monk or a secular priest, came to him, Jov always bowed before him and kissed his right hand. If a deacon came, he honored him by asking him to recite the prayer and he too, like Saint Antony, had his disciple, a deacon, do this.[29]

Jov himself remained as a solitary in that cell at the new skete, ceaselessly weeping and praying that his undertaking might be carried out in accordance with God's will. Sometimes he would come to join the brethren in their rule and at table, at other times they would take his portion of food up to him. At that place he kept nothing at all except what was indispensable for his bodily needs and one small book and an ax with which he prepared the wood he needed for every day.

As soon as spring came, during the great Lent, the *ktytor* sent master workmen. The elder measured the place, then began the foundations for building the church there. Thus, with God's help, it was finished by the Ascension of our Lord. The elder himself served the workers. Himself a man of perfect abstinence, he would prepare meat for them, washing it with his hands and cutting it with his knife and slicing off butter and cheese for them and distributing it. The *ktytor* used to send him everything he needed. When the church was finished, they hastened to move the cells and to complete [the interior of] the church and to prepare the things for its blessing. They worked hard all that summer. Both *ktytors,* Lord Theodore and Peter, told the workers to transport the cells; they themselves lifted them off the wagons

29. Saint Athanasius, *Life of Antony*, 67 (NPNF, 2nd series, 4:214). Antony typifies the attitude of the fathers. If a priest or deacon was among his visitors, John of Lycopolis insisted that he read the customary prayer; see Russell, 54.

and carried them on their shoulders and handed them from one to another as the walls of the cabins were going up and hoisted them up. In this way two cells were put up in one day. They hired skilled workers to roof them. The barbarians then made war. The Poles under Lord Potocki were defeated and *hospodar* Constantine was killed and many people from Pokuttja were carried off in droves into captivity at the beginning of August.[30] The blessed elder told all the brethren to move to the new monastery. He himself took the deacon and went with him to the holy monastery of Univ for the feast of the Dormition of the most holy Mother of God to see about the blessing of the holy church.[31]

Because of the perils at that time they went by a trackless route through the wilderness to the little monastery at Uhryniv and there they stayed for the vigil service for the Transfiguration of the Lord,[†] then again through the wilderness they passed Krylos and Pitryči and went on foot, in great fear, all the way to Univ. There the elder communicated in the divine Mysteries. The deacon wanted to communicate like him, in the manner of the laity. The elder, however, told Father Pachomius, a council monk and his own spiritual father, to examine his conscience. Together with the

6 August

---

30. The Stephen Potocki mentioned here led a Polish expedition to Moldavia against the Turks in 1612; the Turks defeated him and his ally, Constantine Movila, the *hospodar* of Moldavia, and invaded southwestern Ukraine.

31. The Univ monastery church is dedicated to the Dormition; hence for that feast, 15 August, it always drew numerous pilgrims, including clergy and bishops.

elder they decided not to allow Theodosius to put aside his deacon's rank, but told him to celebrate with them. Theodosius was unwilling, since he wanted to humble himself and be the last of all, but in the end he submitted to the will of God and of his fathers and celebrated once or twice.

The elder begged his spiritual father, Pachomius, to bless their church on the feast

14 September of the Exaltation of the Holy Cross,[†] under which title it was founded. With the blessing of archimandrite Isaias and of the bishop of Stagon Abraham and with the latter's antimension Pachomius came with other priests and blessed the altars and the church in honor of the holy and life-giving Cross. On the very day of the Renewal of the Church [of the Resurrection],[32] 13 September 1612, a new church and a new monastery among our people were established, in the reign of king Sigismund III, when the *starosta* of Halyč was Vlodka, under the bishop of Lviv Jeremias Tysarovs'kyj. The next day, on the feast itself, the elder celebrated the feast with those priests, greatly rejoicing spiritually that he had been deemed worthy to see in his lifetime in that remote solitude the bloodless sacrifice being offered for the whole world. So, having entertained them and the *ktytor*, he affectionately saw them on their way.

A Pilgrimage to Kiev

A little later he had a desire to venerate the holy relics of our venerable fathers Antony

---

32. A feast in the liturgical calendar of the byzantine rite.

and Theodosius of the Caves, and of the other holy monks, whose life he strove to imitate. So, with one brother, he set off for Kiev, to the monastery of the most holy Mother of God; with him went also father Herasym, who had taken his place as superior at Uhornyky. Here [at Manjava] he left his disciple, the hierodeacon Theodosius, as his vicar, whom later he would name as superior, as we shall narrate further on. Theodosius in all things pursued a life of *podvyh*, following his elder and teacher Jov and imitating our venerable father Theodosius of the Caves, whose name was given him by God's judgment to bear: in fasting, vigils, in continual attentiveness, in prayer, and in all the works that a new monastery required. Thus he strove to subdue the flesh to the spirit. He encouraged the brethren and organized the community: now there were eight of them.

When the elder departed, as he was journeying on foot through Polissja,[33] he happened to stop at one of the monasteries. They say that the devils cried out loud: 'Why did you bring here an *akuon*, that is, someone deaf;[34] we can't stand him and we can't remain here'. He had so purified his soul and was so filled with grace that he plainly seared

---

33. The region of the marshes on the Prypjat' river between Ukraine and Belarus.

34. Akuon in Greek (ἀκούων) means 'with hearing', but perhaps in copying the particle μη (not) fell out. Earlier Ignatius has told us that in a sickness Jov became deaf, but he must have recovered his hearing, since there is no further allusion to any difficulty he might have had in communicating. The phrase here remains obscure; perhaps the sense is that a saintly person is like one deaf to the enticements of the devil. It may also be connected with popular demonology, according to which a deaf person is repulsive to devils.

and repelled the adversary. After having venerated the holy relics in the holy monasteries and having prayed and spoken with profit to many, he returned to his monastery in the solitude.

A Temptation

After resting a little from his travels on foot he began again to prepare to go to the Holy Mountain, for various reasons. The brethren and the *ktytor* with tears begged him not to leave them. But he spoke out boldly: 'Only if you chain me or if these mountains block up my path all the way to the sky will I be prevented from going to the Holy Mountain.' He forgot the frailty of his nature and how a man cannot move one step from a place against the will of God. He thought, indeed, that it was God's will that he should go, but it was not so, only a temptation that God permitted. He refused to leave off the execution of his plan because he feared human glory [where he was], that it might not deprive him of heavenly. He took with himself one brother, Proxor, after having given over the rule and the government of the brethren to the deacon and having informed the *ktytor* that Theodosius was superior. The brethren accompanied him to the road with weeping and in great affliction, begging God to change his resolve and return him to them.

When he got as far as the town of Kolomyja, from where he wanted to proceed to Moldavia, the Lord in his mercy bound him, not with iron fetters, but with a grave illness, so that little hope was left for his life. He waited a whole week to recover from that illness and to proceed on his way, but the illness only grew worse. He then recognized that the illness had not come by chance, but that God had permitted it to hinder his departure, so that he would not leave unfinished what he had begun, with the brethren not yet made firm. He immediately returned to the solitude to his brethren and as soon as he returned he again became well; he was amazed at God's providence. He again took up his work, clearing off a larger place, building cells, establishing the right order of the common life. He grieved, however, that he had no priest at the church. He often received secular priests, for the sake of the eucharistic liturgy; sometimes he asked for hieromonks from other monasteries to celebrate the Eucharist on some feast. And he prayed to God to grant him to have his own priest.

Theodosius Is Ordained Priest

At that time the brethren of the holy Monastery of the Archangel Michael at Uhornyky, after consulting their *ktytor*, Adam Balaban (may he rest in peace), and with the advice of our father, transferred their monastery to the mountain, moving all the cells and leaving only their little church. There over the gate they built a church of the Ascension of our Lord. In the center of the monastery the *ktytor* wanted to build a stone church, but he put this off, then death took him away. The *ktytor* was anxious to have this church over the gate and another, in the town, blessed, so he wrote to bishop Abraham, asking him to do this.

The elder, with the deacon, hurried on his journey to Volyn', to bishop Paul Kurcevyč,[35] whom he knew and whom he had visited on his way to Kiev. Princess Anna Korec'ka, although she was a fanatical adherent of the Lutheran faith, wanted very much to see the elder. He did visit her; she was very happy to see him and opened her conscience to him. The elder taught her and told her to abandon her damnable heresy, and to submit to the teaching of her bishop and to keep to orthodoxy. She carried this out with alacrity; he commended her to the bishop and departed.[36]

Jov himself wanted to go to the bishop and had a letter of recommendation from the spiritual father of Theodosius. The deacon, however, resisted: he did not want a high post and feared the priestly office. They went to the monastery like this: just then the brethren of the Uhornyky monastery sent a wagon, inviting the elder and the deacon to come for the consecration of their church. The elder took the deacon and they went. There, at the consecration of the church, although Theodosius did not want it, bishop Abraham ordained him priest. This was on the Beheading

29 August   of Saint John the Baptist,[†] 1613. The elder was glad to have at last his own priest and committed all the brethren to him as their spiritual

---

35. Korec'kyj in the text. Kurcevyč was the Orthodox bishop of Volodymyr and Brest, 1620–1625.

36. This incident is documented also in a note of metropolitan Peter Mohyla, AJuZR, 7:66–68.

father. He himself would come to Theodosius for forgiveness and his blessing and would tell him his thoughts.[37] The elder obtained for Theodosius the blessing and authority to bind and to loose from the bishop and from metropolitan Joasaph of Monemvasia, who also blessed Theodosius to be *ihumen*.

ANOTHER TEMPTATION AND TRIALS

A little later a certain archdeacon, Nectarius by name, came from his holiness the lord Cyril, patriarch of Alexandria.[38] The patriarch was then in Moldavia, to see to some matters of church discipline and had some letters about spiritual affairs for the elder, whom he knew well. He added in his letter an invitation to Jov to visit him. 'I want to go to the Holy Mountain,' he wrote, 'and if you would like to come along, and also to go to the Lord's sepulcher, I'll send you at my expense'.

Jov, when he read this, believed this was from God, so he went to the patriarch's envoy, to Halyč. He left the hieromonk Theodosius in his place, but did not reveal his intention to go to the patriarch. In Halyč he took care of

---

37. For the forgiveness and blessing, see the *Testament*, ch.16. On telling one's thoughts to one's spiritual father, see Hausherr, *Spiritual Direction*.

38. Cyril Lukaris, Patriarch of Alexandria 1601–1620, then episodically Patriarch of Constantinople from 1620 until his death at the hands of the Turks in 1638. His tenure in the patriarchal see can be dated from 4 November 1620 to17 April 1623; 2 October 1623 to 14 October 1633; after an interval of twelve days he continued until 16 March 1634; again from 12 April 1634 to 15 March 1635, and finally from 20/27 March 1637 to 29 June 1638.

some church matters with the Balabans, and
they traveled to Ust' and to Domna.

Having taken care of these affairs, he was
supposed to leave the next day for Moldavia;
with such plans he prepared for the night.
God, however, who wanted to hinder this
desire, visited him with an accident. That
night, in the house of Lord Balaban, he went
up into the loft, to rest at night on the hay;
he always used to go away from the others
for the night, either to the hallway or into
the courtyard, on straw, or into the loft, and
so also this time. At midnight he wanted to
arise, as was his wont, but in the darkness he
could not see and fell through an opening.
He happened to fall on the doors to the
cellar and was badly hurt, crushing his ribs,
and lost consciousness. Fortunately, some
persons there heard the noise; they took him
up like one dead and called the Lady Balaban.
She put cold compresses on him, but it took a
long time for him to come around. He was
amazed at God's providence and will and
began to thank God and to pray. *I thank you,
O Lord my God, for all these things, since you
know what is profitable for me. Do not reprimand
me in your wrath nor punish me in your anger.
Have mercy on me, O Lord, as I am weak, heal
me, O Lord, as my bones give way, and my soul
is greatly troubled. There is no health in my body
on account of your anger; there is no peace in my
bones*, with the rest.[†] He prayed to be granted
still some time to live, that he might repent of
his intentions.

Word about what had happened got
around to the brethren; they were deeply af-

A conflation
of the opening
verses of Ps 6
and 37

flicted and quickly sent him one of the brothers, Henadij by name, to serve him in that infirmity. Jov was conducted to the church of Christ's Nativity, where oil was blessed [for the anointing of the sick], and he communicated in the divine Mysteries. He almost died, but the Lord, on account of the benefit to others and because of the tears and prayers of the brethren, granted him life. They then took him, infirm as he was, back to the solitude. The patriarch's envoys, on seeing this, went away saddened.

THEODOSIUS BECOMES IHUMEN

Jov became well again, but not as he had been before. He committed himself to God's will: to undertake the establishment of a community of common life. He did not dispense himself from anything in his weakness, but for the sake of what was profitable for others he paid no attention to himself. Through him the hearts of many persons in many places were raised to God, to imitate the evangelical and apostolic common life. Many of these importuned him. Of these I will mention three, from the monastery in Mozyr:[39] two hieromonks, Manasia and George, and a third, Anfynohen, a deacon, all very faithful and hard-working, who imitated his life of *podvyh*. They stayed there until their death, only eight years, in great humility and ascetic *podvyh*. Others also came; he, however, accepted

---

39. Mozyr is in Polissja, in present-day southern Belarus.

not all, but only a few, and after testing them out. In the case of the three mentioned above, Jov found out after many trials that they had been moved to come by God, so he received them into his community and spiritual union. They brought with them a large amount of gold coins, since their parents were wealthy. Just at that time this came in useful. When Jov saw them stable in that life, he told the *ktytor* to spend the money on church vessels and priest's and deacon's vestments and what was left over for the building of cells. The number of the brethren increased; they were tonsured by the hieromonk Theodosius, whom Jov later made superior, as a man given him by God to assist him.

One time, when the feast of the holy and life-giving Cross[†] came around, Jov went off into the solitude, praying unceasingly and fervently for what he intended to do. When the feast was duly dismissed,[†] he summoned the council brethren and the hieromonks and the deacons, as well as the *ktytors*. Without saying a word to anyone, he prostrated himself thrice before the holy icons, then gave the staff of superiorship to the hieromonk Theodosius and placed the book of Saint Basil in his hands and said: 'As God wills it, I want you to be the pastor and teacher of this flock that God has gathered and will gather in this enclosure. You are a hieromonk and the spiritual father of us all, hence it is right that you should be the *ihumen*. I am old, but I will be your helper until I die.'

Theodosius resisted and did not want this; with tears he pointed out his incapacity. Likewise the *ktytor* and the brethren begged Jov

14 September

On its octave,
21 September

to continue [as their superior]. He replied to them with displeasure: 'What I am doing you don't know, I know. I want to see in deed what I have taught in words.' Jov then fell to the ground before Theodosius. 'I will not rise from the ground,' he said, 'nor raise my face until you do what I ask.' They begged with tears, but he would by no means give in. So, through the pleadings of the brethren and of the *ktytor*, the Lord Peter Ljaxovyč, and Peter Derykyška, and others, he was barely persuaded to accept, albeit weeping. Then the elder arose, prayed, and blessed him from the bottom of his soul and entrusted to him all the brethren. He bowed before the holy icons and sang *It is proper.*[40] Then all the brethren reverenced and kissed Theodosius, as is the custom.

Jov taught the brethren to submit in all things to their superior as to Christ himself, according to the teaching o f the Apostle: *Obey your superiors and submit to them, because they have care of your souls,*† and the rest. Then he said to the *ihumen*: 'May this staff be to you a sign of your office as shepherd, to feed, instruct, and recall to the right path the brethren. May the book of Saint Basil be to you in place of statutes; do all things according to his discernment.'

Heb 13:17

JOV AS REFORMER IN KIEV

Jov, now that he was free from governing, again wanted to be a solitary, so he went off to

40. One of the most common Marian hymns.

the solitude, to the shelter mentioned earlier. In his old age, thus, he passed through the *podvyhy* of the young, living in stillness, suffering hunger and thirst, vigils and standing at all-night prayer. As he was thus passing the winter in stillness, in the *kolyba*, the father archimandrite of the holy monastery of the Caves,[41] together with the leading monks, sent him a letter and a brother with a wagon, asking that Jov set out to them for the sake of God, to establish the common life. With the counsel of the father *ihumen* and all the brethren, Jov left all things and went away with one brother to Kiev.

After his departure the *ihumen* had a proper cell built for him in the solitude where he had lived amidst hardships in the *kolyba*. As concerns the monastery, the brethren gave themselves over to *podvyhy* and spiritual toil, to building up the common life, becoming like their father in all things. They were also occupied with work outside, digging up a place for the orchard, enlarging the place uphill, building cells. The superior received those who came with great desire to remain, and, after a trial, and with the advice of the council elders, he tonsured them. All the brethren, seeing that he was as a superior should be, doing and teaching (cf. Acts 1, 1), submitted to him in all things and worked with great zeal. All together they hewed away the rocks and dragged the logs for building, without sparing themselves. In this way a sufficient

41. The archimandrite of the Kiev Caves Lavra at this time (1599–1624) was Jelisej Pletenec'kyj, who undertook a reform of his monastery.

number of cells were built and the refectory was enlarged. They themselves also excavated a pond and built a small mill.

The venerable elder worked hard, at the holy monastery of the Caves: he counseled, he taught, he instructed, he begged them to observe the good order of common life in church and in the refectory, to love poverty and continence, to shun the passion of self-love, to submit to their superiors, according to the divine Basil. He was hated by many, but with the help of God and of the holy Mother of God and through the prayers of the venerable fathers of the Caves, from that time up to now the fathers there remain observant as much as in them lies.

When Jov returned he found to his joy the superior and the brethren excelling in observance and increasing in number and as if possessing one soul.[†] So he gave thanks to God and went off to the skete where they had built a cell for him; they gave him one brother from the monastery to serve him. Jov again took up a severe life in stillness. Only on feasts and on Sundays he would come to the monastery, to church and to partake of the common table with the brethren. He encouraged all, and his words about patience and obedience were of great profit, then he would go away again.

Cf. Acts 4:32

A New Church Is Built

In this way the number of the brethren rose to forty, and that little church was too small for them. Indeed, the blessed elder had only twelve brothers in mind and a little church for them; he had not wanted to receive more than that. But, as Saint Basil says, it is not without peril to turn away those who come for the Lord's sake.[42] Thus, it turned out to be God's will that this second Theodosius in these latter times should build a large and beautiful church to the glory of Christ our God and to the profit of the orthodox in the Rus' nation, as Theodosius of the Caves had done earlier in Kiev.[43]

So Theodosius, pressed by the tightness of the little church, in particular because visitors too were coming all the time to pray there, in spite of himself came to this conclusion. He wanted to reveal his thoughts, so he went to the elder in the skete and confessed to him what he desired to do. As soon as the elder heard this, he seconded his desire. 'This is from God,' he said. 'Strive to carry it out and ask God for help.' He thus doubly aroused the desire of Theodosius, who began cautiously to talk this over with the council elders, making out as if he feared the work involved, to test their fervor. They, for their part, as if with one mouth agreed wholeheartedly to this. Then he called all the brethren together into the refectory and presented them with his plan and asked whether they were not afraid of so much work. 'Because,' he said, 'not even the smallest plank will fall into its place without our toil; your obedience is

42. Basil, *reg. fus.* 10 (Clarke, 171; Wagner, 59).
43. Saint Theodosius of the Caves built the large Dormition church in the Caves monastery.

needed, and we cannot spare ourselves if we want this. If we are afraid, let's drop this and live with what we have.' All of them, as if incited by someone, began to insist that the plan not be dropped, but that it be begun with God's help.

From this unanimity of opinion, both of the elder and among the brethren, the *ihumen* recognized that it was God's will for the church to be built. He immediately hired workers to cut down trees in the mountains and to make planks from them He himself asked leave and blessing from the elder and the brethren to go to Kiev, to visit the holy monasteries and to venerate the relics of the holy Fathers of the Caves, whose life he strove to imitate, and to visit the monastery of common life in Mežyhirja, with its newly-built church, to begin here according to the same model.[44] Along with that, he hoped on these travels to obtain alms for beginning the construction. Until then they had never kept money, but even if a brother brought some with him, they gave it to the *ktytor* or to the monastery in Uhornyky, and themselves lived in poverty.[45]

He left in his place as *dikej* the hieromonk Manasia and started out with two brothers. When he came to the Caves monastery, the father archimandrite received him with loving-

---

44. The Mežyhirja Savior near Kiev was an older monastery, which from the late sixteenth-century began to revive after a period of decline or stagnation. Early in the seventeenth century three new churches were built there.

45. The author has said above that the *ktytor* used such money for the needs of their church.

kindness and gave him twenty *zloty*[46] for their undertaking. Likewise father Komentarij, the superior of Mežyhirja, received him with love and gave him some *zloty*. So also others, monks and laity, when they found out the purpose of his journey, gave him donations. He took a likeness of the church at Mežyhirja and, after having venerated the holy places and relics and having committed himself to the prayers of our venerable father Theodosius, he returned home.

As soon as spring came he began to busy himself about the construction. Yet in Lent Lord Peter had sent a master craftsman to plane the wood; after Easter, by the providence of God, they found two others, who worked heart and soul and did not want to accept any pay and had to be compelled to take anything. The foundation of this holy church, then, was laid on 23 April 1619,[†] and, as by a miracle, it was finished in just one summer, with the help of God. They wanted to consecrate it on the feast of the Holy Cross,[†] but the elder did not permit such haste, and only the vigil service of vespers and matins was celebrated in it at that time. The eucharistic liturgy began to be celebrated in it on an antimension on Christmas. The full consecration was carried out only on the next feast of the Holy Cross.[†] The blessed elder and the *ihumen* asked the holy patriarchs for their blessing and for the *stauropegion* for that holy church. The ecumenical patriarch, the Lord Timothy[†] of Constantinople, and Cyril [Lukaris] of Alexandria granted this gladly and both

The feast of
Saint George

14 September

14 September
1620

II, 1612–1621

---

46. A polish coin, *zloty*.

sent their blessing and charters. Thus, by the
grace of God, everything was finished and
everything that was needed was had, that
is, beautiful images and priestly vestments,
books, and the bulgarian festal chant.[47] We
all marvel at this and glorify the greatness
of God.

Jov's Last Months

While the *ihumen* Theodosius was still on that
journey, the elder again had to occupy himself
with the Uhornyky monastery. Its *ktytor*, the
Lady Balaban mentioned above, decided that
she wanted to be a nun, so she gave away her
possessions and moved to Volyn', taking with
her the *ihumen*, Father Herasym, since he was
her spiritual father and the guide of her life.
The elder, therefore, was asked to take the
monastery under his care and he could not
refuse. He assumed the charge, dedicating
himself wholeheartedly to it; this cost him a
great deal of work, in his efforts to put things
in order and to maintain the monastery in
common life. Only three brothers were left,
in fact, while the rest had gone away with the
ihumen.

Jov, therefore, stayed at this task almost
two years, acting as *ihumen*. Father Theodosius would send him priests and *poslušnyky*
to serve him, thus making things easier for

47. In ukrainian usage, the bulgarian chant refers to a chant of the eight
tones of the office more solemn than ordinary and used mainly on feasts.
Beauty and devotion of the church services was an outstanding mark of
the Manjava Skete throughout its existence.

him. Among them I too, sinful Ignatius, was
deemed worthy to be of service to him in
that holy monastery of his. The brethren there
increased to twenty. Jov saw himself growing
weaker in his old age and would often say to
us: 'The day of my departure is approaching'.
He was then almost seventy years old. With
the counsel of Father Theodosius, therefore,
he appointed the hieromonk Manasia from
the holy monastery Manjava Skete as their
ihumen. He himself went away into the mountains to his first skete and began to carry out
a great *podvyh*, greater than at the beginning,
with vigils and weeping and sighing and constant attentiveness.

Fathers and brethren, I don't know what
to do. It is as if someone, taking a walk in a
paradise-like garden, filled with many plants
and sweetly-smelling trees with luscious fruit
on them, rejoices at the sight of all these
things and gives glory to God. When he
comes to the edge of this garden and finds
there one of those beautiful and fruitful trees
withering and about to fall down, he is deeply
grieved and forgets his previous joy. In the
same way I, a great sinner, after the teachings
and *podvyhy* of my father, or rather, of our
elder Jov, passing in review his toil-filled
life, was beside myself with joy and was
so consoled that I did not remember my
sorrows. I thanked him who created us in his
Cf. Gn 1:26–27   image[+] and who adorned us with all kinds
of gifts and gave us such a *podvyžnyk* and
teacher in these latter days. He has a witness
in his deeds and in his spiritual fruits, as

the Apostle listed them in pericope 213.[48] My words are superfluous and incapable of expressing the greatness of this man of heroic deeds; rather, my fingers grow stiff and my mind is confused. Now I have come to the edge of the orchard, to the end of his life, and am filled with sorrow, forgetful of all previous consolations.

JOV'S DEATH

He lived only a short time in the skete, with great assiduity, then, on the Friday before Christ's Nativity, he fell sick, running a high fever. On the feast of Christmas his brethren and the *ktytor* Peter visited him. The next day the *ihumen* visited him and begged him: 'Do not leave us, holy Father, for we are all beginners and weak'. He replied: 'This is not my will, but God's'. He then comforted Theodosius, not to grieve nor to be low-spirited, and after teaching him a little, said: 'May God be with you'. Then again he said: 'May your will, Lord, be in all things, as you want it'.

He became transformed, with a countenance of ineffable sweetness, and began to sing the *sticheron* of the third tone: 'I glorify the power of the Father and the Son and sing the praises of the lordship of the Holy Spirit', and the rest, as we have said earlier. He sang

---

48. Pericope 213 = Gal 5:22–26, 1. This is the Epistle reading on the feasts of several great monks, such as Sabas (5 December) and Athanasius of Athos (5 July).

this twice through, then said: 'For two weeks this song has been unceasingly on my lips and in my mind'.

And see how genuine was his observance of the common life, so that even at his end he did not permit himself any relaxation. His *poslušnyk* happened to bring him some dish and, being a simple person, said: 'We made this especially for you'. The elder's zeal was aroused against the server: 'You are urging me to overturn my way of life. All my life I was careful not to seem better than my brother' (for another brother lived with him, the hieromonk George) 'and now, at the end of my life you are breaking my observance' He foresaw his passing away and did not eat that dish.

On Wednesday, on the feast of the holy protomartyr Stephen,[†] he was anointed with the holy oil and he communicated in the Divine Mysteries. He ordered that by no means was his body to be taken from that place, but that he should be buried there. In the night, however, as if through some revelation, just before dawn he sent for the *ihumen*. When the *ihumen* came, Jov asked him to take him quickly to the monastery. 'Since I have toiled all my life in the common life', he said, 'so also I want to die in it; bury me with the other *poslušnyky*.' The *ihumen* was happy to hear this, but it was very difficult to transport him by sled from that solitude. The *ihumen* placed him in his own cell.

On Thursday evening he became very weak. All the brothers were greatly consoled by his coming; they visited him, begging his pardon and asking for his prayers. Jov lovingly instructed each one of them singly about patience, about humility, others about the passions, about purifying the heart from wrath, envy, hatred, and anger, how not to be malicious. The *poslušnyky* he taught to keep to the tasks imposed on them by obedience with diligence and faith and without sloth. To all together he commended the common life in all its aspects, as we had begun to observe it, to be obedient to the superior, and to have love among us. For the rest, they did not make out what he said, as he quoted from the divine writings.

The priests read to him the four Gospels.[49] He saw some kind of vision and indicated it to us: 'Here is a large winged dove'. We all felt that it was the coming of the Paraclete, the Holy Spirit. He reminded everyone about meekness and the monastic *podvyh*. What is more surprising, he named each one by name. At that time the hieromonk Cyril from Zamostja was with us, who spoke to him in Greek, asking his pardon and for his prayers, and Jov likewise answered a few words in Greek.

On Saturday he again asked the *ihumen* to be communicated in the Divine Mysteries; he communicated with great reverence and gave thanks: *Now, O Lord, you may dismiss your servant.*† Then, with great attention and con-

Lk 2:29

---

49. In the byzantine rite there is a special prayer service said at the bedside of the dying. If the death agony is protracted, prayer is continued with other prayers, with the reading of the Psalter, or, especially in the case of priests and monastics, with the reading of the Gospels. Each monastery has its own customs in this regard.

tentment he began to sing, as if greeting some friend: *Leader of the angelic hosts*, repeating this and looking intently upwards and saying the rest of the hymn.[50] We could not make this out, however, since his speech changed before his dying, and his appearance took on an ineffable sweetness.

In this manner he fell asleep, at the time of the evening clapper, while we were singing vespers and only a few brothers were by him, among them his nephew David. He gave up his soul into the Lord's hands quietly and with holy grace and he died without gasping or contortions of the mouth. So he passed to the better life on the Saturday after Christ's Nativity, 29 December 1621. To all of us he caused weeping and joy: weeping, because we were orphaned by such a father and pastor; joy, because it was as if we were sending him ahead to God to intercede and pray for us. We held his funeral on Monday, on the feast of Saint Basil the Great.[†] He was buried in the new church, in the narthex, on the right side.

1 January

Final Invocation

Yet, O venerable and all-blessed, our father and teacher![51] You increased and added to the number of the venerable fathers, for the saints drew you to themselves as one of the

---

50. This is one of the troparia from the matins canon of 8 November, the feast of Saint Michael the Archangel.

51. This entire section paraphrases invocations to the saints in the byzantine office.

same mode of life as they: those who suffered as one who suffered, the crowned[52] as one crowned, anchorites as an anchorite and one who loved poverty and was a perfect follower of stillness. I hold your life and your passing away beyond this world blessed. Blessed are you, for you labored in this temporal life with the hope of eternal joy. Yet, our father, do not forget us, your children according to the Spirit, but as you stand with all the choirs of the venerable fathers and of the martyrs before our Master Christ, pray that we and this monastery may remain unharmed by visible or invisible foes and that we who are weak may be fortified to imitate your life, as we have begun. Instructed by you, after God, we follow the narrow path of afflictions, according to the Gospel, that leads to life. We are, after all, very weak and we are tempted to swerve to the broad, or rather, self-willed road. We beg you, our shepherd, tend us by your prayers in the pasture of the holy commandments of Christ our God: in humility and patience, meekness and love, with common life, in submission and obedience and the labors of continence, watchfulness, prostrations, the mortification of our wills and passions, so that we may honor the *podvyhy* of your life not only with words, but through the imitation of similar deeds. With the monastic common life *podvyh* may we show forth the image of your venerable life. Thus, departing hence, may we be deemed worthy to stand

---

52. That is, martyrs, who have received the crown of victory from Christ.

inseparably with you on the right hand of Christ, by the grace and the love of mankind of our Lord Jesus Christ, to whom be glory, honor, and veneration, with the Father and the Holy Spirit, now and ever and for all ages. Amen.

This life has been written by me, the great sinner, hieromonk Ignatius from Ljubariv, when I was living in this holy Skete cenobium.

THE SPIRITUAL TESTAMENT

OF THE HIEROSCHEMONK THEODOSIUS,
FORMERLY IHUMEN OF THE
HOLY CENOBIUM SKETE,
AS A REMINDER AND WITNESS
FOR THE SPIRITUAL SUPERIOR
WHO IS IHUMEN AFTER ME
AND FOR ALL MY FATHERS
AND BROTHERS IN CHRIST
AND MY CHILDREN
ACCORDING TO THE SPIRIT,
WHOM THE GRACE OF GOD
HAS BROUGHT TOGETHER

I HAVE GIVEN BIRTH by the labor of penitence and have nursed according to the gift of grace in the holy monastery of the Lord's holy and life-giving Cross, in the solitude in which we live. I have written down nothing of my own, but have briefly summed up what is found in the divine writings, recalling especially the commandments of the Gospels and of the Apostles, on which our monastic life is based. Bless, holy father, the reading.

PREFACE

In the name of the Father and of the Son and of the Holy Spirit. Amen. Every father, as long as he lives, is wont and is bound to care about his children, to rear them in obedience and love and the fear of God and when he is about to depart from them through death he often leaves a written testament, instructing his children how they are to live after his death and administer his wealth and his household. In addition, children are entrusted to tutors until they reach full age and reason. Not only parents according to the flesh do this, but also spiritual parents at their departure leave to their children testaments and teachings, as did Theodore Studite and abba Dorotheus and Nil and other divine fathers.[1] We too, ignorant and unworthy as we are, desire to imitate them.

Our blessed elder and father founder, through the grace of the Spirit who lived in him, founded this holy place and established the praises of God in it and taught us daily about the monastic life and the fear of God. He also conducted me, wretched as I am, to the rank of priesthood and committed to me the church and its service and afterwards also all the brethren, to care for them and teach them, making me *ihumen*. He himself did not write anything, but entrusted everything to my sloth. For that reason, I, the hieroschemonk Theodosius, wretched as I am, labored as much as was in my power in this spiritual labor of the holy monastery for

1. There does not seem to be any english or other western translation of the *Spiritual Testament* of Saint Theodore Studite; see PG 99:181318–24. Saint Dorotheus of Gaza did not leave a testament, but he did set down his teaching in writing; see Dorotheos of Gaza, *Discourses and Sayings*, translated Eric P. Wheeler, CS 33 (Kalamazoo: Cistercian Publications 1977). For the testament of Saint Nil Sorskij and his other writings, see G. P. Fedotov, ed., *A Treasury of Russian Spirituality* (New York 1948).

several decades, seeing to the building and introducing good order, with the help of the holy elder. I received the brethren, instructed and taught them, and established everything that was to their benefit, as it was my duty to God and to my father.

Now, since old age is coming and my strength is ebbing away and my infirmities announce the chalice of death, the dreadful judgment of my Master, Christ, threatens me with an examination of the talent entrusted to me.[†] For that reason, while I am still living, I have taken pains to write in brief, according to the ability of my poor intelligence, in charity, a testament for the instruction of the spiritual superior who will come after me and of all my fathers and brothers in Christ, from first to last, for their benefit and salvation. It does not contain words of the world's wisdom or my own reasoning and teachings, but only recalls the commandments of the Lord as they are found in the Gospels, of the holy Apostles, and of the holy fathers. On these commandments our spiritual monastic life is based and established and perfected. Indeed, our way of life and brotherhood, or rather, divine discipleship is founded not on nature, not on flesh and blood, not on human reason, but on the commandments of God and on the Holy Spirit, as the evangelist and theologian[†] writes: *To those who received him he gave the power to be children of God, who are born not of blood nor of the desires of the flesh nor of the desires of men, but of God.*[†]

Such were the twelve Apostles of Christ, then the seventy disciples of the Apostles,

Cf. Mt 25:14–30

Saint John

Cf. Jn 1:12–13

Cf. Acts 2:41–
47; 4:32

then the five thousand who believed, who had one heart and one soul and all things in common,[†] then the multitude [of believers], and from them our monastic fathers and teachers, and from the fathers their children, monks and *poslušnyky*. And up to now the same grace of God and faith and the observance of his commandments founds and raises up churches, monasteries, cenobia, and brotherhoods.

I say this because that same grace of the Holy Spirit has also now—as if in the last times, filled with woes and afflictions, in particular, a decline and persecution of piety and a relaxation of morals and of a well-ordered monastic cenobitic life, when everyone wants to live by his own wit and will, according to the lusts of the flesh and the love of material things—through his servant, our father, raised up from the foundations this holy monastery in this uninhabited solitude for this new Israel, as it raised the tabernacle of old through his servant Moses. As God's glory and light descended and overshadowed that ancient tabernacle, thus showing that it was pleasing to God, so he has honored also this holy monastery with his glory and has multiplied his grace upon it. Its traditions are not derived from the sayings of human wisdom, but from the power of the Spirit, in the fulfilling of God's commandments. Of them I too, although unworthy, remind your fraternal charity, as my spiritual children.

Our monastic life and all our brotherhood consists of four aspects, or rather, commandments: 1) of charity, common concord; 2) of humility and obedience and meekness; 3) of virginity and chastity; 4) of a patient endurance of afflictions and temptations, that is to say, of the Cross.

I have collected from the commandments of God and from the Apostles about these four doings and have written this up in brief, for the perfecting of your brotherly charity. May we, having seen and having known God's love and Christ-like humility and obedience, chastity and patience, through them become like Christ, his true disciples. Thus you will grow more zealous and more desirous of seeking and of working hard to carry out God's commandments, for your salvation. The fire already lit, even if still small, you will fan into a great flame in the furnace of this holy monastery and by the light of your fire you will pass from strength to strength.† Ps 83:8
I could have remained silent, leaving this up to your good will, but, having received the talent of the word, I am afraid of the examination and punishment: *wicked and lazy servant, you should have given my silver to the traders, and I, when I came, would have taken it back with interest.*† David too feared this when he said: *I* Cf. Mt 25:27
will not forbid my lips. O Lord, I have not hidden your reason and your justice in my heart, I have spoken out about your truth and salvation; I have not kept secret your mercy and truth from the great assembly.† Ps 39:10–11

Many of our holy Fathers begin their teaching about the monastic life from the fear of God, others from the renunciation of the world and from not acquiring possessions, in accordance with Christ's words: *If someone*

Mt 16:24; Mk
8:34; Lk 8:23,
conflated with
Mt 19:21; Mk
10:21; Lk 18:22

*wants to follow me, let him renounce himself; and
if you want to be perfect, go and sell your possessions and, taking up your cross, follow me.*[†] Saint
Dorotheus and many others, however, begin
from charity.[2] I too, poor in understanding
as I am, will follow their example, therefore,
and begin from charity, and also humility and
patience, on which, as I know from experience, our monastic way of life stands firm.
Afterwards I shall speak also of other matters
necessary for our life and which we need to
observe.

As your servant and the minister of your
salvation, therefore, I beg you, fathers and
brothers and holy children, strive to keep the
commandments of God and of the Fathers
that I recall to you in these brief chapters, as
you have received them and have kept them
from the beginning. Preserve the evangelical
common life, without possessions, in charity and humility and patience, in watchfulness and prayer, in obedience and meekness,
in silence and continence, in compunction
and tears, and in other *podvyhy*, corporal and
spiritual. In [the observance of these com-
mandments] many of our fathers and brothers who have toiled much, *podvyžnyky*, our
fellow-ascetics, have fallen asleep. Strive to
observe these things with all your soul, to the
very end.

---

2. Here Theodosius' memory lets him down: Dorotheus in fact begins
from renunciation, not from charity; see his *Discourses* in Wheeler. Theodosius probably had in mind Saint Simeon the New Theologian, whom
he quotes elsewhere, see Symeon the New Theologian, *The Discourses*,
translated C.J. deCatanzaro (New York: Paulist Press 1980).

Our nature tends to go from better to worse, from *podvyh* to slackness, because allurements are everywhere, weakness and lust reign, chastity is held of no account, love has dried up, goodness is scarce, there is no one to set things right. These are the last times, the kingdom of Antichrist is spreading, he himself will soon appear, or rather, he is already here, as the Apostle says.[†] For that reason I beg you to cherish this holy community, this love in which the Holy Spirit has gathered you, as a treasure-trove, as a newly-given God's gift. Hold firmly to the commandments of Christ our God, not with fingertips, as if unwillingly or without faith, but with all your strength and all your soul and active charity. If the enemy wars against you and proposes to you to renounce Christ, that is, his love, turn away from him as from a tempter. Answer him, that is, the enemy's suggestion, like Saint Peter: *Judge whether it is right before God to obey you rather than God* (cf. Acts 4, 19). God says: *This is my commandment to you, that you love one another and lay down your souls [for one another].*[†] Suggestions to despise one another and to abandon them are from the enemy. For God's sake, overcome them and remain in charity, concord, community, patiently bearing all things, that we may be crowned by Christ with the crowns of victory, together with all those who through the ages have taken the narrow path of afflictions. Thus you will enter into life and reign together with Christ for all ages. Amen.

Cf. 1 Jn 2:18

Jn 13:34;
15:12–13

CHAPTER ONE
ABOUT CHARITY

In the gathering and union of a spiritual brotherhood and in the formation of the members of Christ's body and in the building up of his Church, as the brethren in Christ are, charity comes first. A community of interests, or holy concord, is the basis, the foundation, the root and the beginning of all of God's commandments.

The first commandment is to love God with all one's soul, with all one's heart and thought; the second is to love one's neighbor as oneself. On these two commandments the whole building rests, as Christ himself said: *in these two commandments are contained all the law and the prophets.*[†] When he established his holy evangelical commandments and gave them to his Apostles he said: *A new commandment I give you, that you love one another.*[†] The bond of perfection likewise is charity, as the Apostle enjoined: *Above all other virtues, seek out charity, which is the bond of perfection, and may God's peace abide in your hearts, in which you were called into one body.*[†] It is the summit of the virtues, according to the *Ladder*.[3] Indeed, God himself is love, as John testifies: *God is love, and whoever abides in love abides in God.*[†] And again: *In this we recognized love, that he laid down his life for us, so we should be ready to lay down our life for our brethren.*[†] The Apostle also commands: *Pursue charity,*[†] and praises its action: *Love is patient, is merciful, love does*

Mt 22:37–40

Jn 13:34

Col 3:14–15

1 Jn 4:16

1 Jn 3:16
1 Cor 14:1

---

3. Climacus, Step 30, the final on the Ladder, on faith, hope, and love, dwells on the preeminence of love.

not envy, does not vaunt itself, is not proud,
is not undisciplined, and does not seek its own
advantage, and the rest. *Love bears all things*
and will never cease, even if prophecies will end,
if tongues will fall silent, if understanding in part
will give way because we will know, and further:
now there are faith, hope, and love, these three,
but the greatest of these is love.† And among
spiritual fruit, the first is the fruit of love. Love
is also like a blazon distinguishing Christ's
disciples, since he said: *By this all will recognize*
you as my disciples, that you have love.†

Cf. 1 Cor
13:4–13

Jn 13:35

All the Fathers recommended to their disciples this virtue beyond all others. Saint
Basil, above all, says: What is more blessed
and what gladdens souls and bodies more
than when persons of various origins and
countries are gathered together, united by
such unity and bonds of love that it seems as
if there were one soul in many bodies. Serving
one another, submitting one to another: this
is how God from the beginning has wanted
us to be. Such persons attentively follow God,
imitating his life in the body, such strive for
the angelic life.[4] And so on. In another place:
Who has love, nourishes God in himself, and
who bears hate nourishes the devil.[5]

For this reason I beg you, fathers and brothers and my beloved children, for the love of
our Lord Jesus Christ, who gave himself up
for our sins, hold to this [virtue] above all and
abide in it, preserve it to the end. Do not prefer

---

4. Cf. the Ascetical Constitutions ascribed to Basil, ch.18; Baguenard,
177.

5. Ascetical sermon V ascribed to Basil (Prologue, V. 3); Baguenard, 51;
Clarke, 143; Wagner, 220.

anything to charity, neither repose nor food nor the soul itself, that is, health and life. This is your calling, which the Apostle calls you to persevere in. *I beg you, comport yourselves worthily of your calling, in which you were called, in all meekness bearing each other lovingly, striving to preserve the unity of the spirit in the bond of peace.*[†] Let us endeavor with all our might to preserve unity and the bond of peace and charity, I beg you, for the sake of the commandments of God and of the Apostles and of the holy fathers, written here. Thus, having lived in accordance with the commandment in charity and community, may we receive the heavenly kingdom, through the prayers of the holy Fathers. Amen.

Eph 4:1–3

CHAPTER TWO
ABOUT HUMILITY AND
MEEKNESS AND OBEDIENCE

The second [virtue] is Christ-like humility and meekness and obedience. He himself says: *Learn from me, since I am meek and humble of heart, and you will find peace for your souls.*[†] And: *He who humbles himself will be exalted.*[†] And: *To the humble God will give his grace.*[†] Christ himself, the Apostle says, *humbled himself and was obedient to death.*[†] And *on whom*, he says, *shall I look, if not on the meek and the humble.*[†]

Mt 11: 29
Mt 23:11;
Lk 18:14
Jas 4:4; 1 Pt 5:5;
Prov 3:34
Phil 2:8

Is 66:2

The meek and humble person is also obedient and ready to carry out all monastic tasks. Saint Basil, in fact, says that the common life is a fishnet, containing virtues of all kinds, first among them a Christ-like humility.[6] In the holy *Ladder* too we read that to the measure that faith blooms in the heart, to that measure the body hastens to carry out its tasks.[7] And again: give the work of your youth whole-heartedly to Christ, that in your old age you may enjoy the wealth of dispassion; what is gathered in youth nourishes and consoles infirm old age. Again: let us, the young, strive vigorously, let us run soberly, for we know not when death will come.

Saint Poemen says that a monk who lives in common life should have these three things: humility and obedience and concern for the general good of the cenobium.[8] Another elder says: the novice has no need of any other occupation except humility, obedience, and bodily toil.[9] Saint Ephrem says that it is the beginning of pride and haughtiness to refuse to work together with the brethren according to one's strength; the beginning of humility and meekness is obedience and manual work.

At work it is necessary to avoid being overbearing, as well as all idle chatter and loquaciousness, but to observe silence and self-restraint with meekness, and to season one's work as with salt with the remembrance

---

6. Discourse on the Renunciation of the World ascribed to Basil (Discours 11); Baguenard, 269; Clarke, 70; Wagner, 29.

7. Perhaps this is a rather general reminiscence of a passage in Climacus, Step 27, On Stillness, p. 271.

8. *Apophthegmata patrum*, alphabetical series, Poemen 103, PG 65:348; CS 59:181.

9. This is a variant of a saying found in the *Apophthegmata patrum*, systematic series, and in other collections of apophthegmata, cf. *Les sentences des pères du désert*, translated. J. Dion and G. Oury (Abbaye S. Pierre de Solesmes 1966) 202.

of Jesus, saying in one's heart: *Lord Jesus Christ, Son of God, have mercy on me.* For the great Saint Basil says: monks should shun all tumult, that is, noisy conversation, because it is often an occasion of sin rather than a good word, and often if we follow this evil road, we fall into foul language.[10] Instead, do as our blessed elder taught us: when it is possible to stop empty talk with two or three words, let one of the more prudent in humility say, 'Forgive me, that I have multiplied words,' and in this way he will put an end to the talking.

Great harm comes from giving one's tongue no rest: it makes our soul empty, it cools the warmth of the grace of prayer, it dissipates the remembrance of God, it drives away the fear of God, it introduces laughter and brazenness, which is the beginning of the corruption of a monk's soul. Saint Ephrem says: if you, monk, see these things in yourself, know that you are utterly lost. I beg you, therefore, drive away this habit entirely. We should speak seemly things to the point and for edification. Let not our holy lips, which pronounce Christ, utter impious and foul words, but only prayer and thanksgiving and what is for the benefit of our neighbor and not for his injury through our passions.

Some are in the habit of speaking to their neighbor about not putting up with difficulties and about disobedience and leaving the monastery. It is the greatest of sins to hurt the conscience of one's neighbor, for even if

---

10. Cf. the inauthentic Discourse on the Renunciation of the World; Baguenard, 266; Clarke, 69, Wagner, 27.

what is said is not carried out, it causes great turbulence. About this the prophet says: *Woe to those who give their neighbor lees to drink.*[†] Hb 2:15
Instead, confirm and console one another in meekness and humility of spirit. For, as it is said, *the Lord is close to the contrite of heart and he will save the humble in spirit.*[†] *I humbled myself;* Ps 33:18
he saved me.[†] Imitating Christ's humility and Ps 114:6
meekness, therefore, let us be humble and zealously obey our *ihumen,* and let us work for the holy brotherhood. May the Lord then remember us in our humility and deliver us from our enemies, impure passions and thoughts, and lead us into peace. Amen.

CHAPTER THREE
ABOUT PURITY OF THE BODY

Purity of the body is necessary for the monk above everything else. It is a supernatural attainment, an imitation of the angels, an abode for the Holy Spirit. Where there is purity there is God. Fasts, vigils, lying prostrate, standing all night in prayer, and work, are undertaken for this purpose, to preserve our body untainted and to escape the devil, who is like a roaring lion[†] and to extinguish the torment of Cf. 1 Pt 5:8
carnal desires and to bridle the fires of youth.

It is necessary, therefore, to keep away from the occasions of sin. The occasions of sin are: wine, women, bodily well-being, and frequent intercourse with seculars. The fathers, therefore, say that monks, especially those who are young and healthy, should not drink wine or other strong drink, but only water, and even this very little.[11] They are to be on their guard against seeing and meeting with women and talking with them, even if the woman is a relative, but to turn away and lower their gaze if they come upon women, even nuns. Saint Isaac says: if you are compelled to speak with women, turn your face away and thus talk with them. Shun nuns like fire and the devil's snare, avoid meeting them and talking with them and seeing them, that your heart may not grow cold in the love of God and be stained with passions. And further on: flee boldness and conversation with young women like the devil's company. Again: better for you to partake of deadly poison than to dine with a woman, even if she be your mother or sister.[12] Blessed Martinian says that it is better to converse with the devil than with shameless women and to be frequently with the devil than with beautiful and decked-out women.[13]

---

11. Cf. *The Philokalia*, translated and edited G. E. H. Palmer, Philip Sherrard, Kallistos Ware, 1 (London: Faber and Faber 1979) 154, 158 (Mark the Ascetic); 2 (1984) 90 (Peter of Damascus); *Les sentences des pères du désert. Série des anonymes*, translated Lucien Regnault (Solesmes 1985) 171. See also E. Kadloubovsky and G. E. H. Palmer, trans., *Writings from the Philokalia on Prayer of the Heart* (London: Faber and Faber 1951) 205. The texts of this anthology are translated from the Slavic version of the *Philocalia, Dobrotoljubie*. The translation of the *Philocalia* cited first in this note is from the Greek version.

12. All these quotations from Saint Isaac are from his Discourse 7, About novices, according to the Greek text; see the French translation of Jacques Touraille, Isaac le Syrien, *Œuvres spirituelles* (Paris: Desclée de Brouwer 1981) 93–94.

13. I have not been able to trace this saying, but Martinian's own experiences are an illustration of it; see *The Prologue from Ochrid. Lives of the Saints and Homilies for Every Day in the Year*, compiled by Nikolai Velimirovic, translated Mother Maria (Birmingham [UK] 1985) pp.168–169 (13 February).

Human nature is fickle; it is heedless of what is good and easily inclines to what is evil. Hence it is well said in the holy *Ladder*: let us hasten to flee, so as neither to see nor to smell the fruit that we have promised not to taste. I am amazed that we should consider ourselves more steadfast than the prophet David; this is impossible.[14] Again: if someone seeks another virtue without this one, he will not see the Lord.[15] Have your children [monks] first of all acquire this, and do not let them see smooth and womanish faces.

Saint Ephrem says: it is a great calamity in common life to have young boys, for even if we talk to them about chastity, our heart is captivated. And Saint Basil says: if you are young in body or mind, shun being with those of your age; on the bench sit far from him, and when you lie down to sleep, your clothing is not to touch his clothing, because the enemy has seared many by this means. And further on: you should not be with him in a place where no one can see you, on the excuse of instruction, because nothing is more valuable than the soul for which Christ died.[16]

Since in this our holy monastery the elder from the beginning permitted us to receive youths into the monastic life, I too permit this, contrary to the custom of the Holy Mountain Athos and others, because of these three reasons. We do not have wine or strong drink; we live in continence and bear the dying of

---

14. Climacus, Step 15; p.180.
15. Cf. Climacus, Step 26; p.249.
16. Discourse on Renunciation of the World, Baguenard, 261, Clarke, 66, Wagner, 23–24.

2 Cor 4:10 Jesus Christ in our bodies.† Secondly, we have been very careful and watchful and taught about this . Thirdly, so as to rear also young and inviolate bodies totally for the service of God and for the dispensing of the divine sacraments, as it has been and is now, by God's grace. In the future too it is necessary to be watchful and not to receive hastily and to have a care about those who have been received. I beg you, therefore, holy children, keep yourselves free from impurity and with all attentiveness and diligence submit to the teaching of the holy fathers and preserve yourselves from small failings, which come from sight and speech, so that you do not fall into great ones. In this manner, preserving purity equal to that of the angels, you will be saved and be with those hundred and forty-four thousand that have the name of the Father of the Lamb written on their foreheads and follow the Lamb and hear the new music and song of those singing before the throne Cf. Rv 14:1–4 and the elders, as John saw in his revelation.† Amen.

CHAPTER FOUR
ABOUT PATIENCE AND TEMPTATION AND
SORROWS THAT COME DURING PODVYH
BY PERMISSION OF GOD AND THROUGH
THE TEMPTATIONS OF THE DEVIL AND
THE CONCUPISCENCES OF THE FLESH

Patience is nothing other than the cross and death, with which we crucify our movements of passion: wrath, anger, and evil lusts, and mortify our evil will and its inclinations for the desires of the world and of the flesh, not allowing it freedom. As Christ himself has said: *if someone wants to follow me, let him deny himself, take up his cross, and then follow me.*[†] Also: *he who does not carry his cross and follow me is not worthy of me.*[†] He reminds his disciples about bearing sufferings patiently when he says: *he who will persevere to the end will be saved,*[†] and, *in your patience you will gain your souls.*[†] The holy Apostle too lauds the patience of the saints: *therefore, let us, who are surrounded by such a cloud of witnesses, putting away pride and sin, which easily surround us, patiently hasten for the podvyh before us, beholding Jesus, the foundation and perfection of our faith, who in place of the joy that was his, suffered the cross and was unmindful of its shame.*[†] He also says: *Suffering leads to patience, patience to testing, testing to hope.*[†] To Timothy he says: *You, my son, have followed my life, intention, faith, patience,*[†] and places long-suffering among the spiritual gifts.[†] The psalmist says: *I waited patiently on the Lord, and he turned his attention to me and heard my prayer and raised me from the pit of passions and from muddy clay,*[†] and so on. And: *in affliction you gave me room; I found affliction and pain and I called upon the Lord's name.*[†]

All the holy Apostles, prophets, and martyrs, and our venerable fathers, the monks, walked this road of affliction and sufferings, carrying their cross. They heard Christ saying: *narrow and hard is the road that leads to life,* and, *strive to enter by the narrow gate, because the wide gate and the spacious road lead to perdition.*[†] He himself left this world carrying his cross. Saint Isaac says that if we go by the

Mt 16:24; Mk 8:34
Mt 10:38

Mt 10:22
Lk 21:19

Cf. Heb 12:1–2
Rom 5:3–4

Cf. 2 Tm 3:10
Gal 5:22

Ps 39:1–2

Ps 4:1; 114:4

Cf. Mt 7:13–14

true road it is impossible that we should not meet with sorrows or that our body remain in one state, suffering no pains or illness. And further on: if something unpleasant comes your way, don't try to avoid it, but accept it with joy, without examining [whence it comes] and thank God that he has sent you this grace and that you were considered fit to undergo this trial for his sake and to be a participant of the sufferings of the prophets and the Apostles and of the other saints, who suffered affliction on this road. Whether they come from other persons or from the devil or from one's body, without God's permission they cannot come.[17]

The divine Paul also testifies to this, calling it a gift of God: *it has been given to us by God not only to believe in Christ, but also to suffer for him.*† And Saint Peter writes: *if you suffer for the sake of justice, you are blessed, you have become participants in the sufferings of Christ.*† And Isaac, further on: from all ages and generations his path proceeds by the cross and death.[18] Again: it is the will of the Spirit that those who love him live in toil; in those who live in ease abides not God's Spirit, but the devil.[19] As one of those who loved God has said: I swear that I die daily.

In this the sons of God are distinguished from others, that they live in sorrows, while the world abounds in food and comforts. God has not seen fit that those who love him find

Cf. Phil 1:29

1 Pt 3:14; 4:13

---

17. See E. Kadloubovsky, G. E. H. Palmer, tr., *Early Fathers from the Philokalia,*. (London: Faber and Faber 1954) 201.

18. *Ibid.*

19. *Ibid.,* 202.

ease as long as they are in the body. Rather, he wants them, as long as they are in this world, to remain in affliction, in hardships, in toil, lacking necessities, in sickness, humiliated, meeting setbacks, with oppressed heart and broken body, rejected by their kin. Moreover, these, that is, the sons of God, weep, while the world laughs, these mourn and the world decks itself out, these fast and the world lives in pleasures.† In them the word of God is fulfilled that says: *in the world you will receive affliction, but you will rejoice in me.*† And: *blessed are those who weep, because they will be consoled.*† And again: *the kingdom of heaven suffers onslaught, and the violent will attain it.*† Saint Basil comments on this: the word of the Gospel calls onslaught violence to the body, like that which Christ's disciples endure in renouncing their desires and bodily ease and in carrying out the commandments of God.[20]

When a person for the sake of God leaves the world, his parents, possessions, glory, and pleasures, and, becoming poor, follows Christ and for the sake of Christ submits to his superior and for the love of God begins also to love his neighbor, to share his life, and renounces his own will for the sake of love of his neighbor and for the sake of obedience; if, besides, he is attentive about his bodily chastity, and for that sake fasts, keeps vigils, lies prostrate, and imposes on himself voluntary *podvyhy*, then the devil, who finds no peace in him, becomes violently angry and assaults him. He raises up insidious war and

Cf. Jn 16:20

Ibid.

Mt 5:4
Mt 11:12

20. Discourse on Renunciation of the World; Baguenard, 270, Clarke, 71, Wagner, 30.

asks him, like Job, of God. Since the body is subject to passions and prostrated by its lusts, he arouses it to wrath, requiting its desires, and, because he wants to attract the soul to his love, he incites a mighty warfare. God permits this, not to give him over to the devil, but to demonstrate the fortitude of the *podvyžnyk* and to increase his glory. He helps him if the *podvyžnyk* gives his will firmly and constantly to God and does not doubt, but perseveres and gives thanks and asks for help in prayer: Do not abandon me, my God, I have done no good before you, but, by your grace, grant me to make a start. And again: *God, come to my aid; o Lord, hasten to help me,*[†] and the other prayers, from a contrite heart and overcome with tears, ever humble, sorrowing, and praying. This is how the man who does violence to himself, who abandons his own will and desire, is recognized, according to Saint Basil[21] God, who sees his patience and pain, strengthens him; he hears his prayer and gives him victory over the devil, whom he shames, but crowns the *podvyžnyk* and sends him his grace for consolation and help and strengthens him for other sufferings.

Ps 69:1

I beg you, therefore, beloved fathers and brothers, be firm and steadfast during the enemy's attacks and assaults and with patience overcome your enemy. With forbearance you will pass the narrow and most grievous path to eternal life, and with patience you will here become fellow-participants of the Apostles and prophets and martyrs in Christ's passion

---

21. Teaching similar to this is frequently found in Saint Basil, but see especially his *reg. fus.* 6 (Clarke, 161–162; Wagner, 245–246).

and there together with them you will enjoy eternal peace and glory. May God grant
you this.

CHAPTER FIVE

ABOUT OTHER OBLIGATIONS AND DUTIES OF
THE MONK AND ABOUT PRAYER AND FOR
WHAT PURPOSE WE ACCEPT THOSE WHO COME

I have spoken about the four most necessary virtues, which are the foundation of
the monastic life and by which we become
monks, according to the commandments of
the Lord and of the fathers. Of this each of us
also makes a promise or vow or oath before
God and the angels and before our brethren.
If we keep this promise, we shall be saved;
if we don't keep it, we will be condemned as
perjurers.

At present we will mention other obligations arising from our vows, which we should
strive diligently to observe: community, that
is, unity, concord. Not only should food and
clothing and other such things be common,
but even our interior: may heart and soul and
mind and moral sense and will and desire
be one, as the spiritual charter by which the
patriarchs gave their blessing mentions and
teaches us, as does also Saint Basil, whose
writings are like the statute of our common
life. Moreover, our life should be according
to the description of the apostolic community
in the Acts: *The multitude of the faithful had one
heart and one soul, and no one called his possessions his own, but they held them all in common,*

Acts 4:32–33 *and great grace was on all of them.*[†] Our way of life, which is evangelical and apostolic, hence based on the source of Christian life, was conceived by Christ and the Holy Spirit and the holy Apostles.

On account of this, let us hold onto it firmly, beloved, as onto a secure life, having good testimony and leading to salvation, in which wealth and private possessions are rejected and opposition is banished. The bond of love is preserved, and where there is love, there is God. *God is love, and whoever abides in love,* 1 Jn 4:16 *abides in God.*[†] We preserve this abiding of the Holy Spirit and of the holy Apostles. By this our life is characterized; to this life we have obligated ourselves by vows sworn before Christ and the Church. Let us observe this to the end. To this life we accept others who come to us; may we never permit this holy life to become other than this.

If a brother should have permission to be away and stay for a time in another monastery (or even in a secular environment), he is to observe the same utter unacquisitiveness and absence of possessions, even to a penny, as it behooves a disciple of the Apostles, under peril of not being saved.

We should also strive to observe fasting, humility, submission, obedience to the superior, who is in the place of Christ, and to all the brethren, according to our promise. Let us endeavor to carry out diligently and attentively, without sloth or laziness or extraneous and vain thoughts, the canonical common rule of prayer and our private rule, that is, psalms, prostrations, bows, and the prayer of Jesus. Even if you do not succeed, and imaginings distract your thoughts and mind, not allowing you to pray purely, do not be downcast or discouraged, but strive with all the greater resolve. This is all God requires of you: striving and faith in God together with constant prayer and trust, and he, seeing your struggles, will invisibly come to your aid. And when he sees that it is useful for you, he will rescue you fully and grant you freedom from thoughts during your prayer. As Climacus says: it is better for novices to struggle against thoughts than against doubts.

Let us especially learn unceasing prayer, that is, the remembrance of the name of Jesus. Standing and sitting and lying, in your cell and in the church, at manual work and at table and on the road, continuously in your mind, with your thought or your lips call out: *Lord Jesus Christ, Son of God, have mercy on me, a sinner.* In this way all invasions and entries of extraneous thoughts and assaults will be cut off. Even if they seem laudable, they are untimely, hence at times of prayer they are to be rejected as an evil. Persevere in this endeavor of prayer at night and by day, accusing yourself in your thoughts and your heart, considering yourself as earth, dust, and ashes, and unworthy of mercy, the greatest of sinners, the most impure of all creatures, and more worthy of damnation than the devils, unworthy to live with the holy brethren, accepted out of pity. However, so as not to despair, say: Yet, by your infinite mercy and divine loving-kindness, I trust to be saved, through the merits of the Son of God, by his cross and his death and the blood shed by him, by which we were redeemed. I have only to believe and obey and carry out to the best of my ability whatever is according to my calling, and to love him as my Creator and Maker and Savior, and in his goodness he will save me freely. This mental doing of love, my beloved children in Christ, I have described briefly. I beg you not to despise this lowly instruction, and God, in exchange for your humility, will reveal to you greater things and grant you to attain them. Amen.

CHAPTER SIX
ON SILENCE OF THE LIPS WITH REASON

Ever preserve silence in your reasonings. This is the root of sinlessness, the beginning of the purification of the mind, according to Saint Isaac.

Our holy monastery combines both ways of life, namely, the apostolic common life and ascetic anachoretism in stillness and solitude. This is because many, both earlier and now, desire and begin that utter stillness and anachoretism, for the sake of pure prayer, then, because of the weakness of our nature and the austerity of that way of life and lack of necessities, or rather, because of the small faith and the infirmity of this present generation, abandon it without having achieved anything and return with shame, having acquired a greater sin. Others choose to live in common, that is, together with many brethren, for the sake of having what is required for the needs of the body. But in its tumult and cares they completely lose their mettle and are overcome by lusts, and all the passions come to life in them, so that, not being able to tame their unruliness, they are either utterly vanquished or abandon this life, exposing it to mockery. People do not understand and do not realize that not the way of life is at fault, but our inconstancy and our lack of observance and of self-restraint.

Still others have devised for themselves a third way of life, without a rule, according to their own will, without any testimony of the divine writings, but out of avarice. Saint Cassian calls them Sarabaiti.[22] About these I don't even want to talk and I urge everyone to be on their guard against such persons.

But, as I said above, this holy Skete community combines both kinds of life taught by the fathers. I beg you, therefore, fathers and brethren and holy children, strive to carry out all the observances of common life, in the good order in the church and in the refectory, finding joy in the common singing and church services, the beauty of the holy church and of the sacred vestments and vessels, as also in a moderate table, with continence. The rest of your bodily requirements, in moderation, you have from God: clothing and shoes, food and drink. Above all, you have the benefit and consolation of a holy

---

22. Cassian, *Conferences*, 18.7; NPNF, series 2 (rpt. Grand Rapids: Eerdmans 1978) 11: 482–483. *Sarabaiti*, or *Sarabaitae*, was the name given to monks who wandered around and lived an undisciplined life. Canon 4 of the Fourth Ecumenical Council (Chalcedon 451) is directed against them. Theodosius calls *Sarabaiti* the vagabond monks of his own day.

and good companionship, brethren who are of the same inclinations and share the same *podvyhy*.

Those also who live according to the second way, in asceticism, solitude, and stillness, keep the anachoretic way of life and silence of the lips. Everywhere, in the cell and at manual work and outside the monastery, observe silence and attentiveness, I beg you, with the remembrance of Jesus. Have a care to show regard for one another and remind each other not to multiply words, that our hearts may not grow cool and our prayer disturbed, and the rest that is written in Chapter Two.

I have kept silence about this for a while, since I saw how new all this was for you at the beginning and how you were not yet accustomed to the solitude and our way of life, and how much work there was at building the monastery, and I myself was immersed in work and with many preoccupations. Now, by the grace of God, you have grown to maturity and have become accustomed to our way of life, and the building is finished, and I could take a rest and finally I have a brother to whom I can pass on the cares and management of the *ihumen*'s office. I beg you, clasping your feet, let us amend, let us be watchful and observe silence, humility, devotion, patience, obedience, a vigilance concerning chastity, prayer, vigils, attentiveness, despising visible things, desiring the things above, where our

Cf. Col 3:1–2 life is,[†] to where our fathers and brethren have passed, the firstborn of our way of life, and where we too will soon follow them.

Let us cease dreaming about wandering

as poor pilgrims, for this is instead cutting oneself off, disobedience, and a transgression of our vows. Let us rather think of death, the grave, and the terrible day of the last judgment, the revealing of our deeds and an examination of our vows, the kingdom of heaven for *podvyh* and chastity and eternal torments for sloth and carelessness. Let us think of this at all times and by this means repent in our hearts and humble our spirit. But let us wholeheartedly bear the toil of our two-fold life, and in that way you will also receive a two-fold recompense from Christ, together with the Apostles and ascetics and hermits and all the venerable fathers, through their prayers and those of all the saints. Amen.

CHAPTER SEVEN
ABOUT THE ABSENCE OF ANGER AND RANCOR

In a life such as ours, of obedience and physical toil in external works as in internal services, in common tasks and in church services, when those who sing and others are a long time on their feet, together with our fasting and abstinence and the absence of special dishes to fortify anyone, for the sake of the common bond, there often arises murmuring and anger and rancor.

I beg you, for God's sake, may this not be. Bear these things patiently, for the sake of the bond of charity, and expect a recompense or prize for this from Christ God in the future life, and do not seek to be requited here. If someone has a need or is weak and requires to be fortified, and it is not a case of the passion of gluttony, let him go humbly to the *ihumen* and tell him his need. The *ihumen* will give his blessing that he drink something or eat, if there is only one meal that day. But everything is to be done with the blessing of the father *ihumen* and in the refectory. Nor is any brother to take scandal at this or to desire the same thing for himself or condemn a just decision and a need that has received a blessing.

If the *ihumen* does not grant it, do violence to yourself and accept it, and do not become angry, because the passion of anger is very destructive. Similarly, if you ask the *econome* or the brother in charge of the storerooms for something and he does not give it at that time, don't become angry, but bear it, recalling Christ's poverty and your own cross. So with regard to everything else that you need and don't receive, bear it without ill-will and without anger, and thus you will attain perfection.

It may be that some brother has spoken harshly or sharply to you, or some superior has reprimanded you, whether you were at fault or not, and you are grieved and passion seizes you and you start thinking: why has he not reprimanded me the way a monk should? he could have rebuked me with brotherly love; but I'll talk to him in the same fashion, I'll repay him with the same coin. No, Christ's servant, my beloved brother, don't say this, but withstand at that time and say: I have sinned, it's my fault. Even if I have not sinned this time, nevertheless, at other times, or rather, at all times I sin against God, and God has sent this for the healing of my soul. Even if he rebuked me, as Saint Dorotheus writes, he is my brother. How many times Christ met with insults for my sake and did not grow angry, but bore it patiently. Since I am his disciple, for my sake and for Christ's sake will I not bear a word from my brother? And pray like this: Lord Jesus Christ, have mercy on my brother and help him, and help me by his prayers.

If the temptation returns, repeat this prayer, even many times. In this way, by the grace of God and your resistance, the wound of anger will quickly be healed, and you will progress in not bearing ill-will and in purity of heart and will reach perfect love, which is the crown of all virtues. The other passions should be opposed in the same way, that is: gluttony, lust, sadness, accidie, above all vainglory and pride, by praying to God and cutting them off at their entrance and enticement and doing the contrary, if we want to reach dispassion and with it obtain the kingdom of heaven in ourselves, and especially to have Christ the King come to dwell in us.[23]

I implore you, fathers and brothers, with all diligence take pains about each one of these. Since I revere the fathers' words and teachings, I don't want to write about everything. Pray also for me, in whom all passions come to deed, that by your holy prayers, holy children, we may receive forgiveness of them from God. And may God grant you not only

---

23. This traditional teaching on the passions, or passionate thoughts, derives from the teachings of Evagrius Ponticus; see his *The Praktikos and Chapters on Prayer,* translated John Eudes Bamberger, CS 4 (Spencer-Kalamazoo: Cistercian Publications 1970).

to avoid all sinful deeds, but to pull up by the
very roots the passions and their thoughts,
by the prayers of our holy fathers and of my
holy father Jov and of all the saints. Amen.

CHAPTER EIGHT
THAT IT IS PROPER TO BE
MODERATE IN FOOD AND DRINK

From the first this holy monastery has followed an ascetic way of life, as is proper to
sketes and as is taught by the elders. Going
beyond the custom of other cenobia, such
as the Athonite and ours, our monastery accepted the custom of not using butter and
cheese and wine. This was established at
our founding and is observed until today.
This is very good and beneficial, especially in
these latter times, when food among monks is
highly regarded and pleasures rule and gluttony knows no bounds and little attention
is given to chastity and the overcoming of
passions. On account of all this, God, through
our holy elder, has given us this as something
extremely beneficial. Let our ascetic rule or
statute of fasting remain always like this, to
confine ourselves to grains and fruit and vegetables grown from the soil, as it was before
the flood, so in our monastery it is up to now.

*Let us also say something about moderation in
these things.*

In all actions the divine writings call virtue
the mean. This is what is beneficial, while

extremes, that is, indigence and overabundance, are harmful. For Climacus says: do not incline either to the right or to the left, but go by the royal road.[24] Saint Basil too commands us to moderate abstinence according to our physical strength.[25] Abba Dorotheus talks about the need of having a measure in eating, that is, if you eat your prescribed measure and see that your strength is not restored, add a little more, but if you eat your prescribed measure and see your strength restored, fix a definite measure, and thus you will eat according to your need.[26] Peter Damascene also advises to diminish or add the measure of food according to one's strength,[27] and the other fathers write about this moderation. They command us to flee pleasures and the passion of incontinence and gluttony like the abyss of sin and foulness. Our master Christ himself also admonishes us: *Do not let your hearts grow heavy with much eating and drinking;*[†] and, *woe to you who are filled, because you will go hungry.*[†] Therefore I too, in this my holy monastery, according to the discernment of the holy fathers, choose what is moderate and pass it on to my children and brothers in Christ.

Lk 21:34
Lk 6:25

---

24. I cannot find this in Climacus, but this is a common teaching; cf. letter 16 of Evagrios Pontikos, *Briefe aus der Wüste,* Sophia 24, translated Gabriel Bunge (Trier: Paulinus-Verlag 1986) 227; Dorotheus of Gaza, Discourse 10 (Wheeler, 165).

25. See, e.g., Basil, *reg. fus.*, 18, 19 (Clarke, 182–184; Wagner, 273–277).; *reg.*, 126, 128, 135, 139 (Clarke, 277, 278, 279, 281); cf. the inauthentic Ascetical Constitutions, ch. 4 (Baguenard, 137–148).

26. Discourse 15 (Wheeler, 217); cf. his *Life of Dositheus.*

27. See his writings in *The Philokalia*, vol.3, translated. and edited G.E.H. Palmer, Philip Sherrard, Kallistos Ware (London: Faber and Faber 1984).

It is true that at first with the blessed elder we followed an extremely severe regimen in food and drink, eating only once a day, except on Saturdays and Sundays and great feasts, and the measure [of our food] was smaller, and we had fish and oil only rarely on Sundays and great feasts. But since the brethren have increased in number, and among them there are many who are still young and weak, and I saw that they were fast losing strength, which was not being restored, and many were becoming infirm and could not carry out common tasks, that is, the monastery's services, then, according to the counsel of the holy fathers and of Saint Basil, I mitigated this a little for the sake of rest and strength. The blessed elder was still living then and he gave his blessing to this. In this my writing, hence, I transmit this to our fathers and brothers and faithful children in the Lord, so that they remember and observe it also in the future. Let nothing be changed for the sake of vanity or of pleasure-seeking, but only when a need arises, when it will be up to the judgment of the *ihumen*.

CHAPTER NINE
ON FOOD IN THE REFECTORY
AND THE NUMBER OF DISHES,
HOW THIS IS TO BE EACH DAY

Pentecost

From the Sunday of Easter, that week, and the week of the Descent of the Holy Spirit,[†] and the two weeks after Christmas, and the fastless week before Lent, and Cheesefare week, we permit two meals every day, with fish and oil, if there is any; only on Cheese-fare Wednesday and Friday, one meal, after Vespers.[28] From the Sunday of Saint Thomas[29] until Pentecost, on Mondays, Wednesdays, and Fridays one meal a day, with honey and gruel, as is the customs for fasts; on Tues-days, Thursdays, Saturdays, and Sundays, two meals, with oil. If there is fish, it is per-mitted to serve it, but in our solitude fish are scarce, and, in any case, ascetics should not seek this out too much. For dinner there are always two dishes, for supper one and a side-dish, that is, a relish of whatever is available, either cucumbers or mushrooms or left-overs from the earlier meal, if there are any. If there are none of these things, let some beans be cooked or a little cabbage, or some dry roots, one measure for four. If there is only one meal, then likewise let there be two dishes and a relish.

During the fast of the holy Apostles,[30] on Mondays, Tuesdays, and Wednesdays, two

28. Fasting is mitigated for monastics and abolished for everyone else, meat being allowed every day in the first four weeks mentioned here; dairy products are permitted every day in the last (Cheesefare). The fastless week before Lent, which Theodosius calls by a popular name, *serkyzka*, falls three weeks before the beginning of Lent; Cheesefare week is the last week before the beginning of Lent. The dietary instructions here and in the following Chapters are entirely in the tradition of hesychast spirituality, adapted to what was available in the Carpathian Mountains. Although Theodosius does not cite them, his teaching can be usefully compared with that of the monks Callistus and Ignatius of Xanthopoulos in their 'Directions to Hesychasts', in Kadloubovsky and Palmer, tr., *Writings from the Philokalia on Prayer of the Heart*, 202–208.

29. The octave of Easter Sunday.

30. The fast of the Apostles begins on the Monday after All Saint's Sunday (the octave of Pentecost) and lasts until the feast of Saints Peter and Paul, 29 June; it is thus of variable length, depending on the date of Easter, and hence of Pentecost.

dishes without oil and a relish, on Thursdays twice, with honey or a gruel, two dishes in the morning, in the evening one dish and a relish. On Fridays it would be good to keep a fast without cooked dishes, but it is the custom to stew dried fruit, only do not oversweeten them, on account of the fast. It is proper to eat very little on Fridays, so that one's stomach feels affliction, and we recall the Lord's sufferings. If there is work to be done, and the brethren will be fatigued, then on Tuesdays there can be a second meal; this is up to the *ihumen*'s discretion. The other fasts, of the most holy Mother of God and of Christ's Nativity, are to be observed in the same way.[31]

In meat-eating weeks throughout the year, in the same way on Mondays, Wednesdays, and Fridays: one fast meal, with two dishes, with gruel or honey, and a side-dish; on Tuesdays and Thursdays [at dinner] two dishes, one with oil, the other dry or with a gruel of seeds or poppyseeds, and in the evening one dish sweetened in the same way and a side-dish; the same on Saturdays and Sundays, with fish, if there is any. If there is sufficient fish, fresh or pickled, then the father *ihumen* may give his blessing to have it served also on Thursdays, to fortify the brethren. If there is no fish, then even on Saturdays

---

31. The fast of the Mother of God, in preparation for the feast of Dormition, 15 August, lasts from 1 to 14 August. Advent, the fast before Christmas, begins after the feast of Saint Philip the Apostle, 14 November, and goes through 24 December. Theodosius says nothing specifically about Lent because its practice was well known: all lenten days are fast days, as are Wednesdays and Fridays throughout the year.

and Sundays one has to be resigned to go without it, not murmuring against the superior, or rather, against God, but giving thanks, whether there is or there isn't any. Also on great feasts that have a vigil we permit the same as on Sundays. If the saint [of the day] is celebrated with the *polyeleos* and doxology,[32] we permit the use of oil and two meals; even if it falls on Friday serve a [second] small meal in the evening. The brethren should have leave to fast as they wish; it is better not to go [for the evening meal]. Similarly, on Tuesdays and Thursdays, when there is a meal in the evening, it is permitted to omit one meal. Everything, however, is to be done only with the blessing of the spiritual father or of the *ihumen*, not out of self-love and according to one's own opinion. Saint Basil, in fact, says that if someone follows his own inclination and does not submit in this, he sins more than he does good by fasting.[33]

Similarly, if someone on a certain day wants to abstain from a particular dish, he is to tell his need to the father, who will give his blessing. Fasting, says Saint Basil, is not just as everyone decides for himself, but according to need.[34] If we approach food in this way, we will keep to the mean and to moderation. I entreat you, holy fathers and brothers, may these things be kept in all particulars unfailingly and always.

---

32. These are saints' days celebrated with greater solemnity than usual, but not with a vigil.

33. Basil, *reg.*, 128, 137, 138 (Clarke, 277, 280–281); Prologue V (Baguenard, 49–50; Clarke, 142; Wagner, 219).

34. Basil often teaches this; see note 25 above, also *reg.* 16.

Chapter Ten
Let us also say something about occasional fasts and permissions

If there should be some need for someone or for all to fast beyond what is customary, that is, if some visitation of the Lord comes, war or famine or epidemic or persecution by heretics, or else, to prepare oneself better for the Divine Mysteries, and the father announces for all a fast beyond what is usual, the brethren should accept and observe it with faith and love, like the Lord's fast, for as long as he determines. Likewise, if he imposes a fast beyond what is customary on a brother for a penance, the latter must observe it exactly. This is called an occasional fast.

About occasional permissions

If the *ihumen* sees the brethren occupied with heavy work or if they are preparing for a fast or for some undertaking, he may add a little something, that is, another dish beyond the usual food; this is to be done according to his discretion. Likewise, when there is a commemoration of a deceased brother,[35] or if some honored guests come, according to his discretion something may be added, or a second meal may be served on what is normally a fast day, but not on Wednesdays and Fridays during Lent. These last are to be observed inviolably, with only one meal a

---

35. This is an agape, called *tryzna* in Ukrainian, observed most often on the occasion of a funeral, but sometimes also on the statutory commemoration of the deceased on the ninth or fortieth day after death or the annual remembrance.

day. Similarly, if some brother is setting out on a trip before a meal is served and something separate is given him, this is all to be done according to the *ihumen*'s judgment. These are called unusual occasions.

CHAPTER ELEVEN
ABOUT SICK BRETHREN WHO CANNOT GET UP

A brother who is sick and cannot get up is to be served food and drink and everything else he may need in the infirmary, so as not to grieve him. When he requires something, he is to be humored, because to grieve a sick person offends his Creator. If during his affliction he does not find anyone to assist him, the person who neglects to take care of the sick, as it says, will not see light. If a sick person is able to walk about, but the refectory food is not sufficient for him, he should present his needs truthfully to the *ihumen*, not falsely, for all lying is from the devil, and may the Lord destroy all who speak falsehood.[†] The *ihumen* will tell the servers to prepare whatever is necessary beyond the customary, on account of the illness. The sick brother is to be seated separately, or else his food is to be sent to the infirmary, but everything is to be done with the *ihumen*'s blessing.

Cf. Jn 8:44; Ps 11:4

CHAPTER TWELVE
ON DIFFERENTIATION OF
FOODS IN THE REFECTORY

The superior is also to see to it that in the refectory one dish is always moist, the second solid, one sour and the second sweet, on account of differences in natures and needs. If some brother naturally does not eat some food,[36] but there is another dish, let him take that and make up for the other with bread. If there is only one dish, which he all his life does not eat, then let him be given something else, according to his need. Of the foods and vegetables that are available, let everything be given in rotation; when they are gone through one by one, start again. However, we have vegetable broth practically every day, and also buckwheat porridge.

On drink

The drink appointed for monks at all times is water, but among us also vegetable broth or juice. Thirst is useful for the monk beyond all other toil, says Climacus.[37] If God from somewhere should send us beer, let it be taken in moderation and at proper times: on Tuesdays, Thursdays, Saturdays, and Sundays, and on feasts, one or two glasses a day. On Mondays, Wednesdays, and Fridays, water, unless for the sake of some heavy work or if a brother is sick, as we said in Chapter Ten and Eleven, as necessity requires, with the father's blessing. Mead or brandy may be taken only if some Christ-loving person should send it or for stomach illness, or, if we have it, for a feast after some great fast, but we should not strive to acquire it. Rather, we should recall the prophet's ashes and tears:

---

36. Today we would say: has an allergy to some food.
37. Climacus, Step 6; p.133,

for I ate ashes like bread and mingled my drink with weeping, and tears were my bread day and night;[†] and Christ's gall and vinegar.[†] Let us also recall the daily hunger and thirst of all the holy and venerable fathers. Thus, we shall not greatly desire such food and drink, if we recall these exemplars.

Ps 101:9; 41:3
Cf. Jn 19:29; Ps 68:21

Chapter Thirteen
On differentiation in bread

The usual bread is always to be rye. Wheat loaves may be served on occasion, if God sends them to us through someone, or we ourselves bake them for some feast. We may have wheat rolls for Sunday; they are to be plain, and not multiplied, not overlarge, for the two meals. Thus the brothers will have consolation, but will avoid satiety. If someone has not had his fill, let him make it up with rye bread, avoiding both gluttony and satiety. As for fancifully baked goods, that is, filled or layered pies, we are to shun them utterly, so as not to fall under the condemnation of John Chrysostom, who in his homilies brands seculars by calling them pie-makers and gluttonous eaters. And it is up to the *ihumen* occasionally to give consolation to the brethren with these things, not for the latter to seek them out. Moreover, everything is to be done with an eye to what we receive and to our storerooms. If God, to try us, sometimes grants us to feel want, we should be ready to bear the lack and hunger thankfully.

CHAPTER FOURTEEN
ABOUT SWEETENING WITH
HONEY AND ABOUT OIL

Sweetening or seasoning with oil should be done in the pot, so that all get the same dish, with oil or dry, from the superior to the last monk. The same is to be followed with regard to all pleasurable foods, fresh fish, pickled fish, wheat bread. The servers are in conscience bound to divide everything equally, even for the novices who have not been tonsured. If one kind of wheat buns or of fish does not suffice for everyone, then, as there is need, the novices may be given another kind, so as to carry out this requirement.

CHAPTER FIFTEEN
ON CLOTHING AND FOOTWEAR

Clothing should be, as Saint Basil says, the same for all: simple, coarse, and long-lasting. The only difference and selection to be made is that a big size is inappropriate for a small person, or a small size for someone big.[38] The same goes for footwear.

Since our clothing is not acquired from the same batch or all at once or is all of the same workmanship, it may give rise to envy. But every ill-will and injustice in thoughts is condemned. The *ihumen*, together with the *econome* and the brother in charge of the storerooms is to decide about this. They have been

---

38. Basil, *reg. fus.* 22 (Clarke, 188–189; Wagner, 281–284); *reg.* 168 (Clarke, 291).

judged fit to manage these things and are concerned not to offend any brother, according to their conscience. Whatever clothing, due to our poverty, falls to the lot of someone, even if it be of the poorest quality and old, he should receive it humbly and with thanks and not murmur. Warm clothing too, that is, sheepskin coats, cannot be new for everyone; there are always many old ones, and only two or three newly gotten, so they cannot be all alike. I implore you, therefore, fathers and brethren, holy children, accept this patiently, without long faces and without murmuring, according to the judgment of the superior and be grateful to God that in such a solitude and in such dear years we are not left naked and famished. Let new clothing, for the sake of decorum, serve the altar for us, on the brethren who are ordained, and let us share the old articles and bear Christ's poverty and humility and patience, which are the mediators of our salvation, not passion, to the concupiscence of which we cater with clothing or food. Let us rather imitate the poverty of the holy fathers and the holy Apostles.

For the holy Apostle Peter says to his disciple Clement: Don't you, Clement, understand my life, that I live only on bread alone and olives and poor herbs, that I have old clothes for my garments and that I don't require anything else.[39] And all the saints

---

39. This comes from the Pseudo-Clementina, an early christian romance in the style of a collection of writings purporting to be by Clement of Rome. For the text in an english translation, see *The Ante-Nicene Fathers*, 8 (rpt. Grand Rapids: Eerdmans 1978); the incident quoted occurs on p.158 (*Recognitions*, 7.6), 293 (Homily 12.6).

passed their lives *in sheepskins and goatskins, indigent, sorrowing, suffering insults, of whom* the world was not worthy.[†] Father Isaias says: do not be vain about your clothing, but recall Elias's[†] cloak, Isaias's[†] sackcloth, and do not forget the Baptist's garment of camel's hair. And Saint Ephrem says that whoever loves bright robes is naked of divine robes. The love of fine clothes has nothing in common with the kingdom of heaven. And Saint Simeon the New Theologian says: we, miserable, full of passions, after having left great and splendid things and entered a monastery, fix our love on soft clothing and leather belts and knives and sandals and coverlets and sweet foods and drinks and apples and luscious fruit, through love of which we are totally estranged from Christ the King and become his enemies. The holy fathers say that the demon of lust observes the garments of a monk: if he has a better one for the sake of show, this is a sign of lust.

I cite the testimony of the holy fathers so that you, fathers and brothers, recalling it may repent and will be satisfied with the old and worn-out that the monastery and these times provide. Thus you will bring peace, not trouble to the superiors who decide about these things and you yourselves will be saved, as those who keep the commandments of God and of the fathers. Amen.

Heb 11:37–38

Elijah's
Isaiah's

Chapter Sixteen
About not talking after compline

The holy Fathers and the rules of holy and ancient monasteries prescribe that after

Compline monks are not to converse with one another at all; they are not to stand about the monastery for the sake of conversation or gather in the cells. Only the *ihumen* may speak if some need of the monastery should arise, but even that only in the cell, for the sake of good order. Neither may one drink water, exception being made for the sick. Compline has been established by the holy fathers as the key and closing of the entire day. And if someone, being human, happened to sin that day, then with contrite heart and humility he makes prostrations before the presiding priest, as before Christ himself, confessing his deeds, words, and thoughts.[40] If someone is conscious of having sinned in some grave matter that day, he is to confess separately and receive forgiveness; without confession and without forgiveness he is not to go to sleep, for fear of death, since many have fallen asleep in the evening and have not risen in the morning. *In what I shall find you*, the Lord says, in *that will I judge you*. There is no other consolation at the moment of death than repentance and confession.

Thus, after the forgiveness, all are to go to their cells, as to a tomb, without speaking to a brother in the cell, except to say briefly and very softly what is necessary for the cell. Nor are they to sing out loud or to bustle about noisily. They are to be occupied with prayer and watchfulness and be sober in stillness, with heartfelt contrition and with tears, working with their hands, and be attentive in

40. Byzantine Compline concludes with a rite of forgiveness conducted by a priest. This is a generic confession of faults. Theodosius mentions this, then goes on to speak of sacramental confession.

stillness to their reading. Having kept vigil in this manner a little, they are to go to sleep, granting a little rest to their bodies, as nature requires and so as to prepare themselves for the morning vigil. Receive this my brief reminder with love and observe it. May God be with you. Amen.

Chapter Seventeen

That it is improper for monks
to go outside the monastery
without the superior's blessing

Without the superior's blessing, even if there is great need, the brethren are not to go outside the monastery.[41] When it is necessary, then it is to be done with his blessing, since even a good thing becomes evil when it is not blessed. Hence, if even for a good and necessary reason a brother should not go out without a blessing, what can we say about an evil reason, to deride, laugh, engage in empty talk? obviously this is perdition. When a monk becomes careless and begins to wander aimlessly outside the monastery without the superior's blessing, then the devil begins to give him chase, either to entrap him into sin or to give him over to death in the enjoyment of his disobedience, as the *Gerontikon* writes.

A certain elder lived fifty years without ever going out of the monastery and observed everything proper to a monk. The devil grew envious of this and tempted him to go out of

---

41. Cf. Basil, *reg. fus.* 44 (Clarke, 217–218; Wagner, 320–322).

the monastery without a blessing. He caught
his foot and pierced it on a stone and lost so
much blood that he died. When the superior
was told about his death he could not understand how the adversary had managed to
beguile the monk to go out of the monastery
without a blessing and ordered all the brothers to pray with him for the deceased brother.
They prayed day and night, and a voice came
to them: do not count him who broke his vow
as one of the brethren, but drag him by a rope
tied to his feet and throw him into a ditch.
This they did.

For this reason the Fathers prescribe that
such a person is not to be buried nor to have
the eucharistic sacrifice offered for him, since
he broke his vows, which he made before
angels and men, to renounce the world, to
remain in the monastery until his last breath,
and to observe obedience to the superior until
death. How terrible is this judgment of God
and of the holy fathers against those who are
so bold as to do this. We have no fear and not
only dare to go out of the monastery without
a blessing, but, contrary to our promises, to go
away even to foreign lands and across the sea
and ultimately to death without the blessing
of our *ihumen* and our spiritual father, like
many who have already met that kind of
death.

Behold such foolhardiness and lack of understanding. I beg you, therefore, fathers and
brothers, flee self-willed action and insub-
missiveness, and especially disobedient going out without the superior's blessing, like
corruption and the sting of death. Be vigilant

until death, so that a double death may not
overcome such a transgressor of his promises.

Chapter Eighteen
About the election of the *ihumen*

After my death the foremost brethren, priests,
deacons, and *economes*, are to choose an *ihumen* from among themselves, especially from
among the priests, whomever they see to
be the most zealous, humble, meek, long-
suffering, self-restrained, loving the brethren,
and, above all, loving God and fearing God
and keeping his commandments and loving
the monastic rule and keeping the customs
and traditions that this holy monastery has
observed from the beginning.

He is then to be announced in the larger assembly, as useful and necessary for the monastery and for the salvation of the brethren.
They are all to give their agreement to his
election, avoiding dissension and conflict. If
someone out of a passion of wrath does not
consent, the foremost brethren are to reprimand him and entreat him. If he does not
submit, he is to be ignored, as causing dis-
cord, and those who have better understanding and hold the higher posts and are of the
majority are to be followed. Whoever is chosen by them is to be chosen by all.

He is to be elected for one year, according to the order of the Holy Mountain Athos
and church law, that is, our patriarchal charter. May he be blessed with the blessing
of God and of his holiness the patriarch of

Constantinople and of our council, on account of the prayers of our holy father, our founder and elder, the venerable Jov, and by the prayers of all our holy fathers; may God's grace be upon him. The father vicar is to give over to him the staff and the seal. Then, according to custom, the kiss of peace follows, and all the brothers render their respect and submission.

They are to obey and honor him as their superior and father and *ihumen* and pastor, who takes Christ's place. He is to administer and govern everything with the council of elders, according to custom, the way this holy monastery began, neither discarding anything nor adding anything, but if anything has been neglected, he is to correct it. All this is to be done with the advice of the elders and of the father vicar, who is to be first after the *ihumen*. He is to preserve and keep everything that is described in this our testament for the benefit of those who will come after us.

He and the council brethren are to recall when the year is up. If it is agreeable and useful for the monastery and all the brethren, he may be asked to continue laboring for a second or a third year in this holy obedience of superiorship, and he is not to refuse this charge, which is useful and salvific for him and for all in general. If something displeasing or not useful is observed in him, as, for instance, if he should begin to overturn existing and established custom, or fail to see to the good order in church and in the refectory and not to observe moderation and to disregard and despise the admonitions of the council elders, such a person should be submitted to this same judgment of God and church law. The holy council is to be convened even after half a year, not waiting for the year to be up, and the staff and seal are to be taken from him in due manner in council by the father vicar or the foremost hieromonk, or he himself is to restore them, just as he in due manner assumed that holy office. Nevertheless, nothing is to be done out of jealousy or groundless hostility against him, nothing without a trial and a long period of patience and of fervent prayers to God, because time and prayer can test everything. The grace of God and the prayers of the holy fathers and of our lowliness be with you. Amen.

Chapter Nineteen
About the election of the *Econome* and the other ministers and their services

In the same manner that I have spoken about the election of the *ihumen*, the *econome* too is to be elected among you, an experienced and faithful brother, also for one year. The *econome* is called curator, administrator, or overseer, under whose care is this holy common household. The *econome* should be God-fearing, faithful, industrious, keeping track of income and expenses, with good judgment about material things, administering them not as if they were his, but God's, with all care and friendliness and the fear of God attending to everything, with a sense that God oversees all. As Saint Basil says, carry out the duties of your service properly and assiduously, as one who is serving Christ, *for cursed is everyone who does the Lord's work carelessly.*[42] Be on your guard against evil negligence when you have to occupy yourself with tasks that seem lowly, since, with God overseeing all, nothing is lowly or of little importance that is done for God's sake.

Jer 48:10

The *econome*, therefore, should have great care, likewise the other servers, that is, cooks, breadbakers, those who have charge of the refectory, that they not infringe on something of authentic customs by their weakness and thus become a scandal to those who will serve after them. They are not to eat or drink anything more than the brethren, even if they happen to eat separately after all the rest have eaten; they are to eat what the *ihumen* has blessed to be eaten by all the brethren. Nor are they to have anything extra in clothes or footwear. For this reason, I beg you to endeavor to act blamelessly, carrying out everything as it is written. And not only the ministers themselves are to observe and keep what has been written, not to eat or drink anything, but also those who are under their charge and instruction, that is, those who are being trained to follow in these services.

The *econome* is to look after all the food-stuffs in the storeroom conscientiously, that is, wheat, flours, all kinds of seeds, that nothing spoils through carelessness, that moths and mice do not damage it. If something is scattered by the servers, this should not be overlooked, but care is to be taken over every

42. Basil, *reg. fus.* 34 (Clarke, 200–201; Wagner, 298–301).

grain or trifle, since what is received of God's things is never something little. He is to reprove fearlessly with loving words the baker or cook, saying: Brother, how can you be so indifferent about your conscience as to deal carelessly with the things or foods that are given to us from God's hands for the support of those who serve him. He himself is to watch out, as is written in the Gerontikon. An econome rebuked the cook about two grains of lentils or beans that had fallen and gave him a penance for having been careless in the service of God.[43]

So also in other things, especially honey, oil, pepper, and other condiments, he is to admonish the cook that there should always be some for the needs of the brethren, but there should be no superfluous and unnecessary condiment, as that would be sin and ruinous passion. And he should not allow the father *ihumen* to ask about it, for the fathers in their writings say that every use beyond necessity is sin and deprives man of divine providence. We, on the contrary, are not able and not prepared to suffer want. For this reason I beg and charge you, as my beloved children, to see to these things diligently, as received from the hand of God and entrusted to us by God so that we may take care of them and administer them to God's children and brothers. *As much as you did for one of these least of my brethren you did it for me*, says Christ.[†]

Cf. Mt 10:42;
18:5

How terrible it is to carry out carelessly and without the fear of God and the advice and

---

43. See Cassian, *Institutes*, 4.20 (NPNF, 2nd series, 11:225).

blessing of the superior the service entrusted to one, be it as *econome* or as refectorian or as cook, is described in the life of Saint Euthymius. A brother who served in the refectory without the fear of God became possessed by the devil and for many days was tormented by him. The brethren prayed for him to God and to the saint at his grave. The saint then appeared to him and said angrily: do you believe now that nothing can be hidden from God? do you see how terrible it is to be careless about Christ's work? do you understand that in the monastery everything is holy and consecrated to God and those who are careless of these things go to perdition? That brother repented, and the saint cured him.[44]

A *Paterikon* recounts the following. A brother asked father Zeno: tell me, father, how can I know whether my service is acceptable to God? The elder replied: the first sign for him who serves is a good intention and the love and fear of God; the second sign is humility towards all, thinking that one serves not men, but angels and God and as if standing before the throne of Christ, according to what God said, *where I am, there will my servant also be;*† the third sign is gentle words, speech without murmuring, heartfelt sighs, the shedding of tears, the fear of God, the desire of future good things, care about what has been entrusted to one so that nothing be

Jn 12:26

---

44. The life of Saint Euthymius is recounted by Cyril of Scythopolis, *Lives of the Monks of Palestine,* translated R. M. Price, CS 114 (Kalamazoo: Cistercian Publications 1991). For the incident referred to here, see pp. 69–72.

done out of time and that there be nothing in excess of need in material things, but that everything be done with faith and the fear of God. If you see and feel this in yourself, your service is acceptable and agreeable before God and angels and men. The contrary will have the contrary recompense.

For more about these services, read what Joseph the Muscovite writes more fully in chapter six.[45] This little reminder I have sketched briefly, out of love, as something that those who are to come after us, I beg affectionately, should read and recall my love and unworthy labor in the obedience that was confided to me concerning you. And in requital for that love each one is to strive to carry out these things in deed and not to forget me in your holy prayers when I have departed. May Christ deem us worthy to stand inseparably on his right and to inherit the heavenly kingdom. For his is the glory and the power, with the Father and the Holy Spirit, now and ever and for ages of ages. Amen.

CHAPTER TWENTY
ABOUT THE OTHER MINISTERS
AND THEIR SERVICES

The other ministers—the refectorian, the cook, the baker—it is useful to change every

---

45. The reference is to Joseph of Volokolamsk (1439/40–1515), see *The Monastic Rule of Iosif Volotsky*, edited and translated David M. Goldfrank, CS 36 (Kalamazoo: Cistercian Publications, 1983; new revised edition 2000).

quarter year, as is the custom, on account of the tiresome work of these duties and so as to train others and drive away their tedium. The person in charge of the storerooms and the rest are to be appointed for a year, like the *econome*, so that a frequent change of persons does not bring confusion to the good order of the church. About the good order in church, standing, attentiveness, and singing, entering and coming together, about the fear of God and silence and the rest, I refer you to the book of Joseph of Moscow, by whose efforts this is described. Above all, see to it that nothing of authentic and well-ordered customs that have been introduced and confirmed in this monastery is undermined. But correct unwillingness and indifference and lack of fear and work out your salvation. Glory to God for all things, who orders everything to our benefit.[†] Amen.

Cf. Rom 8:28

[FINAL EXHORTATION]

In this my testament I have briefly compiled and written up all these prescriptions and duties from the evangelical and apostolic commandments of Christ God and the example of his life and the rule of Saint Basil for a reminder to my fathers and brothers and children according to the spirit, which they are obliged to keep. But beyond all this, what I write in my testament needs an inspired teacher, judge, and guardian, and a constant administrator, that is, *ihumen*, a pastor and true leader and superior for the flock, to recall to it God's commandments and my testament

according to God. The written word, as one
wise man has said, is a dumb philosopher,
who understands much, but cannot tell people what he understands. In the same way,
writing contains the understanding of many
things, but cannot talk of itself. For this
it needs a servant and leader, to carry out
in deed for the disciples what has been
bequeathed, so that the written word may
become a salvific deed.

Hence I, a sinner, according to my ability have toiled in this holy monastery; I
have taught, instructed, tended as a shepherd, measuring myself against the commandments of God and of the holy fathers,
as much as it was possible to fit this in at our
beginnings, when I was more occupied with
external matters, in building. Now, mindful
of the grave and my death, while my memory
is still good and my mind is sound, with
my own hand I write this testament to my
children, how they are to live in the house of
God, this holy monastery. I place God himself
as helper and his most pure Mother as pro-
tectress and the Holy Cross as guardian and
mediator of this holy monastery and of those
who live in it.

In this my testament I ordain before God
and write down with my hand that two
things be ever preserved and kept. By them,
after my departure, this monastery is to be
governed, maintained, and last eternally,
with the help of God and the prayers of
the holy fathers and the blessing of the holy
patriarchs, whose blessing we have in their
letters, and by the prayer and blessing of my
lowliness.

The first matter is this. I wish to establish, while I am still living, my honorable brother and faithful and dearest son according to the spirit among the hieromonks, the lord father hieroschemonk Dorotheus as my successor, that is, the heir of my post and office. May God's blessing and mine be upon him and may my father's[46] prayer be with him for ever. May Jacob's blessing come upon him and may the spirit that is in me be doubly in him, as Eliseus received after Elias, and as Joshua after Moses, and as Solomon after David in right judgment, so that what I conceived in pain and gave birth to in the spirit he may multiply in deed and make fruitful in salvation.

To him I confide before God and the Church my blessing and place and the monastery and all the brethren, especially all the labor and care that I bore. To the brethren I enjoin that they submit humbly with all their heart and all their soul and render him obedience and compliance as they have rendered it to me and that they listen to and honor him as their superior and as God's minister and as my and the elder's successor and heir and follow him in all things, on account of the commandment of God that says: *he who hears you hears me,*[†] on account of my commandment, if they want to be together with us at the right hand of Christ on the day of judgment and have the succor of our prayers.

Lk 10:16

He too owes it to God and to me and to the holy monastery not to excuse himself from this, but, taking on himself the burden of

---

46. That is, Jov's.

obedience, he is to strive with all his might
to live the common life according to the
commandments of God and of the fathers
and of Saint Basil, and to preserve and firmly
guard all the traditions and customs of this
holy monastery and not alter the good order
of the church and the refectory, and to observe
unaltered the abstinence that we received
from the first, as God's law, and to hold to and
observe the decisions of his fathers after God,
and to enjoin upon the brethren these things,
and to teach, instruct, and correct the brethren
in a spirit of lowliness, with infinite patience,
and to receive and judge their consciences, to
bind and to loose. Everything that I have had
may he too have from God and from me; I
leave and give it to him in this my testament.
May God's blessing and ours be with him
forever. And not only on him, but may the
same blessing from God be on those who will
come after him, the second, the third, by the
judgment of God and of the brethren. May
the Lord out of Sion bless them now and for
all ages. Amen.

The second thing or matter of this holy
common life is this. I establish a council of
twelve brothers and elders, which number
is to be statutory and always the same. If
one of them dies or can no longer continue
because of illness or ceases to be a member
for some other reason, another is to be chosen
in his place, as the Apostles chose Matthias,
to complete the number of the disciples.

These twelve older brethren have this for
their first duty: In conscience before God
and before the spiritual father and before the

gathering of the monks they are to promise in word, as if taking an oath before the holy icons and the holy cross, to be as it were our patrons, to observe all faithfulness and justice towards God and towards the brotherhood of common life. Putting aside all vacillation and doubts, they are faithfully and patiently to suffer, bear in patience, take counsel, intercede in assaults of the devil and bear the weakness of the weak brethren, according to the Apostle, and thus fulfill the law of Christ.[†] With such faith and trust they are to labor and are to remain unfailingly ever present in this holy monastery until death or until being driven away by heretics. Like common fathers to the brotherhood and faithful elders and advisers and sworn councilors of the father *ihumen*, the superior over all, they are to deliberate together with him, both about the bodies and the souls of the brethren. They are to look after and guard good order in the church and in the refectory, as well as income and expenditures, and monastery goods, those that belong to the church and those of ordinary use, movables and eatables; they are also to judge of monastery affairs and whether it is necessary to send someone somewhere. And one of them is to be sent for the sake of fidelity, so that good order and decorum and abstinence be observed on the road, so that God's glory and the good name of the holy monastery not be besmirched by our unseemly behavior.

From among these sworn elders the *econome* and the brother in charge of the storerooms are to be chosen and appointed

Cf. Gal 6:2

for the established period, and also the ecclesiarch, that is, the superior of the church.
This establishment or order of council elders
has been introduced from the first, from the
times of the blessed elder Ezechiel,[47] and has
been kept through all the years that I have
been *ihumen*, with the first members of this
new foundation. I, lowly, did even more, I
encouraged and confirmed, taught and instructed them, and trained them as beginners,
for this salvific toil and pious cares. Now, by
the grace of God and the prayers of the holy
fathers, this monastery has increased in size
and the brethren have multiplied, and this
council has been tried out already for many
years, and it has been shown to be by God's
help of general benefit to the brethren and to
the whole community.

After much toil and after my inattentive
life the warrant of death and my departure
from the body approach. By the will of God I
deliberate about you, my children, and about
the holy monastery and about the evangelical
life, as a founder of this holy place; as your
predecessor and ancestor, I write my spiritual
testament for you, my children. I ask and
implore you with tears that the resolutions
I have set down in my testament be unwa-
veringly kept and unfailingly observed and
last forever. This refers to those twelve foremost brethren, sworn-in, faithful to our way
of life. The rest of the brethren are to hold
these elders in honor and obey them as lawful

---

47. That is, the founder, Jov Knjahynyc'kyj, who took the name Ezechiel
at his profession on Mount Athos, see *Life*, 3.

arbiters and spiritual counselors and superiors of the holy monastery. The father *ihumen* himself is to hold them in greater honor
and esteem and not ignore their counsels and
advice, but receive with love what they say
and what they advise and confirm it with his
prudent decree.

They, for their part, are to hold the *ihumen*
as Christ among them and honor him with
the honor that befits a father and obey him
as their pastor and head and heed and not
despise his word. They are to see that the
brethren honor and obey him. In his cares
they are to console him, like a man, and
inspire him with confidence. They are to
be guardians of religious justice in general
and always humbly insist on it in council;
finally, they are not to let anything that is
customary to be undermined, only they are
to admonish suitably, not pounce on anyone
in an authoritarian and offensive manner.
Reproof is permitted from those who are
older in age and understanding, according
to Saint Basil, Chapter 50.[48] If what deserves
correction is rebuked, we benefit him, he
says, and ourselves because of him. May
murmuring and judging never occur, for this
is a source of anger and hatred and scandal.

The father *ihumen* himself is not to grow
indignant over being admonished about matters and actions that concern the common life,
nor be resentful or angry towards them, as
often is the case under the impulse of passion.
Nor is he to vaunt his superiority, saying:

---

48. That is, Basil's *reg. fus.* 50, (Clarke, 222; Wagner, 327).

look who's talking! But he is to listen humbly to what they have to say, for the sake of the bonds of love, and, having patiently heard them out, promise to correct himself. Or else, with prudent speech, he is to give an account and lovingly show before the council that his action was blameless, thus pacifying them, not raise a storm over the matter, under pain of the fathers' and our blessing being withdrawn.

Likewise, if the *ihumen* accuses a council elder or all of them and scolds him loudly or exclaims that he cannot put up with him any longer, do not be grieved or saddened or leave that life and council on account of it. But humble yourself like the least and recall the threat of the dread Judge, according to the *Ladder*. Rather, as an example to the younger, you are to fall down and ask forgiveness and remain at peace at such a time. You may explain yourself before him alone or in the presence of all, but it is not well to argue obstinately, showing your will and pride.

I ask and implore you, my fathers and brothers, about this, since I have had experience of this for many years. May you carry on the work of God and the administration of his house, which is the holy Church, for the sake of your and your brothers' salvation. Because of the lack of humility and patience both in those who govern and in those who are governed life everywhere has degenerated and the apostolic and brotherly community and the bonds of the spirit have been rent, and the holy monastic life has taken a course of self-will. May it never happen among you.

I ask for the Lord's sake that for some private reason or trivial offense or for the sake of your ease you not break away and leave the holy community. I do not give my blessing for this and do not forgive it and call such a one before the dread judgment and place a curse upon him.

Only if after many years of toil and service in the common life and common laudable cares, with the blessing and judgment of the council elders, someone wants to lead a life of stillness and pray to God for his sins with weeping, it is not to be denied him to live like that either for a time or until death. He is to be supplied with food and other necessities from the monastery; may such a separation be blessed. He is to confirm the common and brotherly life with his counsel and word, but especially with his prayers he is to benefit the weak among the brethren, who toil in the community.

And again I beg you, fathers and brothers, and say together with Saint Paul: *I, an old man, beg you to walk as worthy of the calling to which you have been called, with all humility and meekness, with patience, bearing with each other in love, striving to preserve unity of the spirit in the bond of peace.*† For without keeping to your vocation and without humility and meekness and without patience and love it is impossible to preserve spiritual concord and the bond of peace. Strive, therefore, to live in love, according to my poor-witted prescriptions, for, as the Scriptures say, *he who abides in love abides in God and God in him.*† And in return for your obedience and humility

Cf. Eph 4:1–3

1 Jn 4:16

and patience, may the help and grace of God and the prayers of our humbleness and the prayer and blessing of my father, the elder Jov, remain with you forever, Amen. And may you be successful in your undertakings and *podvyhy* and may the Lord's blessing be with you forever. Amen.

After my departure those twelve council elders have for all times the authority and power from the Lord, and my blessing to choose an *ihumen* from among themselves. When they elect and announce someone to the brethren, he is not to try to excuse himself and oppose the general verdict, but he is to accept it as an obedience imposed by God and strive wholeheartedly to carry it out. So also as regards the other servers: these elders, in council together with the father *ihumen*, are to assess and choose them, namely, the econome, the cellarer or keeper of the storerooms, the brother in charge of the refectory, the cook, the brother in charge of the laundry, and the ecclesiarch, and the other servers. Those chosen by them are not to try to get out of the work and cares that are for God's sake, but receive them with faith and with zeal, as if serving Christ himself, according to his words: *whatever you did for one of these least of my brethren you did it for me.*[†] And, *whoever wants to be greater, is to be a servant to all,*[†] and, *whoever humbles himself like a child will be greater in the kingdom of heaven.*[†] Of that heavenly kingdom may Christ deem us worthy, through the prayers of our holy fathers. Amen.

Mt 25:40
Mt 23:11
Mt 18:4

After my departure, what I have prescribed is to be frequently read in council, as a reminder for the council brethren and the father *ihumen*, that they may be mindful of their duties. Together with that, here is what they are to see that the brethren observe:

1. As soon as the clapper is struck, each one is to put aside what he is doing in his cell and prepare to go to church; before the clapper stops all are to be together in church.

2. All together, as if with one body, are to bow in church, touching the ground with their hand, fervently with prayer.

3. Good order in church is not to be disturbed in anything: singing, bell-ringing, incensing, the lighting of the candles, moving about, unless there be a great lack of something or of celebrants.

4. When the bell is rung for some common work, all are to heed it and come immediately; if someone is unwell or is occupied, he should say so, but not stay away on his own out of laziness.

5. They are not to walk around the monastery or go into a brother's cell, especially if there are guests around, without the *kamelaukion*.[49]

---

49. The *kamelaukion* is the monk's cap; at that time in Ukraine it had a form rather like a skullcap.

6. They are to remain in their cells, be occupied with manual work, and observe stillness.

7. Without a blessing they are not to give away anything they have made or any vessel, under pain of remaining without a blessing.

8. They are not to put up anything in their cells according to their own fancy and without a blessing.

9. They are not to roam around the cells without a real need and they are never to take anything from another's cell without a blessing when the brother is not there.

10. When they take any implement, of wood or of iron, as soon as they are done using it they are to return it to the same place from where they took it, not somewhere else, so as to avoid disorder, under pain of spiritual penance. If they borrowed it from a brother they are to give it back to the same brother.

11. Clothing and footwear are not to be chosen according to one's fancy, but accepted according to the judgment of the superiors.

12. Elders who are sent out on obedience, together with their brother, are to guard against scandalizing people in the world in anything; they are not to enter any building where people drink and are to avoid any drinking.

13. Fast and abstinence are not to be neglected until the end of one's life, both on the road and in the monastery.

14. Those who return from a journey are to give an account of it, according to Saint Basil,[50] and are also to give an account of the money and ask forgiveness from the spiritual father for their transgressions, according to their conscience.

15. All those who serve and those who do manual work are to be very careful about and take care of implements and all common things, as offered to God; they are not to damage them or throw them about any old way, under pain of penance.

16. If accidentally someone damages or breaks something, he is bound in conscience to report this act at once and to ask forgiveness.

17. After Compline they are not to talk or make noise, as said above.

18. They are to be repeatedly reminded that fire is to be kindled in the cells with great caution and kept low.

19. Superfluous things are not to be kept in the cells, but given to the superior or to the storerooms.

This is the end of the testament of our father Theodosius, the *ihumen* of the Skete cenobium and its founder.

---

50. Basil, *reg. fus.* 44 (Clarke, 217–218; Wagner, 320–322).

REGULATIONS, OR STATUTE, OR RATHER, RULE OF THE ASCETIC MONASTIC LIFE

At the Skytyk by the Church of
the Most Pure Mother of God,
where there is also a chapel of our
venerable father Onuphrius the Great

1 N THE NAME OF THE FATHER and of the Son and of the Holy Spirit, may [this *skytyk*] grow firm and develop for the prospering of those who want to live following the narrow path. Amen.

By the grace of God, our skete way of life, which was initiated by the blessed elder, our father, for two or three persons, has developed into a cenobitic way of life for many, where the requirements of good order and active work, talking and the care of common and necessary interests have multiplied, on account of which mitigation has to be permitted in food and stillness and the rule, or attentiveness. For this reason, I, the lowly superior Theodosius, sorrowing for the stillness that was and the straitness of the narrow and most grievous road that I tasted at the beginning, have renewed this second abode of asceticism, the *skytyk* begun by our venerable elder, and assign to it the church of the most holy Mother of God. Four or six brethren are to live there, imitating the primitive asceticism and observing stillness, under the authority and blessing of the father *ihumen* of the great monastery and by his provision. One among them is to be superior, if there be a priest or elder, who is to admonish and have care of the others. All are to submit to him, obey him, and receive his blessing and permission for everything. He, on his part, is to give an account of everything to the *ihumen* and take his advice.

[1] *First of all*, they are to observe stillness, keep silence with their lips and never converse with one another. In only four matters may they speak:
1. to sing and to pray, to call out to God;
2. to read to oneself or to talk to another for <spiritual> profit;
3. to instruct or reprove a brother lovingly;
4. to speak about things necessary in life, what to do and how.

[2] *About the rule of prayer in church.*
The rule of prayer in church is to be in common, without singing: Vespers, Compline, Matins, and the hours. The liturgy, when it is possible, once or twice a week, is to be sung softly and devoutly. If there is no singer, the cherubic hymn is to be read thrice in a drawn-out manner and in unison, twice before the entrance and once after. Similarly the communion verse, but with faith and the fear of God.[1] For Vespers, the strophes are to be taken from those that are available, sometimes in

---

1. This direction echoes the priest's words in the byzantine eucharistic liturgy, with which he invites the faithful to communion.

the monastic manner, sometimes the akathist, sometimes of the church.[2] If there is an Octoechos or Menaion, the service is to be taken according to the proper order.

At Matins the psalter reading and sessional hymns are to be taken according to custom, then one canon from among those that are available, for six or eight troparia. If it is a Sunday or great feast, then everything in the Menaion is to be read devoutly, without haste;[3] the *polyeleos* is to be read, the versicle may be sung. The troparion and the doxology may be sung, for spiritual consolation. *God is Lord*† and the *Glory* after the strophes are to be sung.[4]

Verses from Ps 117

[3] *About daily food and drink.*

There is to be one meal a day. Mondays— one dish is to be *kysil'*,[5] the other with gruel. Tuesdays—likewise one dish dry, the second with honey or gruel; the same on Thursdays. On Wednesdays and Fridays, dry food or stewed fruit and parboiled beans, with a side dish of whatever is available, radishes or cucumbers, mushrooms, or some fruit, always with moderation and avoiding satiety, so that we may not lose the benefit of stillness. On Saturdays and Sundays and on great feasts, two meals: one dish dry and the second with

2. Here directions are given what to take at Vespers if all the books are not available.

3. The services for great feasts, as also the services for Sundays of the eight tones, were collected in separate books, hence were more readily available than the services of the sanctoral or daily cycles.

4. For an explanation of the byzantine office, see Robert Taft, *The Liturgy of the Hours in East and West* (Collegeville: The Liturgical Press, 1986).

5. A gelatinous dish made from fruit and farina.

oil, and in the evening one dish with honey or gruel or a side dish. In the weeks without fast, two meals or a side dish with oil, if there is any; nevertheless, on Wednesdays and Fridays one meal. Drink is always water or vegetable broth, and even this with moderation; beer or fish are never to be sought.

On feasts or on a Sunday, if we come to the monastery, we eat what they have, or when the *ihumen* and brethren in their charity visit us and send something along, we partake of it.

Fasting may be increased for a time, out of zeal or love, with the blessing of the *ihumen* or the spiritual father. If someone becomes sickly or afflicted, he is to be taken into the monastery, to obedience in serving many brethren, and another is to be received into the *skytyk* in his place.

4. *About clothing and footwear.*

Clothing there should be poor and worn and coarse, given from the monastery. In the cell and outside, especially in the summer, the monks are to go barefoot, like the ancient anchorites.

5. *About the rule of prayer in the cell.*

In the cell, the rule of the Psalter two times a week,[6] and a *paraclesis*[7] or other canon, one every day. Evening and morning three hundred or more prostrations, everyone according to

6. That is, the entire Psalter, with accompanying prayers, was to be read through twice every week.

7. Here, this refers to a petitionary canon, a hymn of nine odes, addressed to the Mother of God.

his strength, but with his spiritual father's knowledge. Six rosaries of the Prayer of Jesus a day and six at night are to be recited, with the utmost attentiveness and heedfulness, devoutly, with contrition of heart. The monks are to remain in uninterrupted prayer, that is, always have their minds fixed on the Lord Jesus, and sitting, standing, lying, walking, and working, they are unceasingly to strive to keep their minds on and to say: *Lord Jesus Christ, Son of God, have mercy on me, a sinner.* As Saint Basil says: Fasten your fault in the remembrance of him. And as Saint Ephrem says: In toiling toil hardily, that the suffering of vain toil may pass you by.[8] And as Saint Chrysostom says: May your heart consume the Lord, and the Lord your heart.[9] And other holy Fathers speak about this.

6. *About manual work.*

Manual work is to be whatever one knows: to make wooden crosses or spoons, or things out of wool, in silence, with the memory of Jesus, after reading the third and sixth hour and until the ninth hour. The ninth hour is always to be sung after midday, before the meal. After the meal, again manual work or chores in the cell, that is, preparing the wood and tidying outside, then Vespers. After celebrating Vespers, a brief pause, or water may

---

8. I have not been able to locate this in Ephrem, but the same phrase, ascribed to Ephrem, is quoted by Gregory of Sinai (14th century) in his 'Instructions to Hesychasts', in Kadloubovsky and Palmer, *Writings from the Philokalia on Prayer of the Heart*, 93.

9. This is quoted by Callistus and Ignatius, 'Directions to Hesychasts', *ibid.*, 223.

be drunk, then Compline is to be read. After Compline the monks are not to gather or talk among themselves, not even about necessary things, but everyone is to recite his rule of prayer, and be attentive, and meditate on the grave and death. If there is need, manual work may be taken up by candlelight, for one hour, in silence. Then, however, after a prayer, they are to go to sleep and give nature its due. Then, again, rising soberly they carry out their obligations, the prayers of the midnight office and the prostrations, presenting their first thought to God, offering him the compunction of their hearts and humbling their spirit before him. Then they are to come for the common prayer of Matins [and the first hour], standing attentively and listening to the reader. The reader is to read slowly, clearly, and devoutly, as if conversing with God. After Matins, if it is still early, they may take up manual work. If it is already dawn and there is light, they are to recite their rule of prayer, with prostrations, the rosary, and the Psalter, until the third and sixth hour, and take up manual work only after these have been read.[10]

The brother who is carrying out the service of cooking and the refectory service is to receive the blessing [from the superior] and go about his duties with attention so as to be ready on time and come with the other brothers for the ninth hour and for every other rule

---

10. Private prayer was put off until there was light because it included spiritual reading, cf. *Life*, sec. 8. While prayers could be said from memory in the dark, for reading light was needed, while candles, scarce and costly, were mostly reserved for the church.

of prayer, unless something unexpected turns up. One's handicraft is to be turned in on Saturday or Sunday to be sent to the monastery, so that the father *ihumen* may dispose of it, and to pick up the required food supplies from the monastery. If the *ihumen* with the council should need one of the brothers of the *skytyk*, to send him for supplies or for some other common service for the monastery, the brother is not to use his stillness as an excuse, but recall that he who obeys is greater than he who fasts.[†] He is to serve out the time needed for his obedience with faith, so as not to be deprived of the common prayers and blessing and possess blamelessly the peace of stillness.

Cf. 1 Sm
15:22–23

If the brethren live according to this rule, everything will be of benefit, and the bonds of love will not be transgressed, and the praises of God and prayer will be multiplied. Pray for me and work out your salvation. Amen.

GLOSSARY

Antimension   (from the Greek, literally, 'in place of the altar'), is a cloth with relics sewn into it and consecrated by the bishop. Today it is generally found on all altars in the byzantine tradition, but strictly it is necessary for the celebration of the Eucharist only on altars not consecrated by a bishop.

Archimandrite   A title of superiors of some large or important monasteries, installed in a specific liturgical rite.

Asceticism   In the texts, *postnyčestvo*, which in Slavic literally means 'fasting', but refers to all ascetic practices. The collection of Saint Basil's ascetic writings, for instance, is called in Slavic the *Book on Postnyčestvo*.

Attentiveness   This and the closely related terms *watchfulness, vigilance, sobriety* (q.v.) refer to virtues central in hesychast spirituality. They describe the attitude of keeping guard over one's heart and mind, of dispelling evil thoughts at their first emergence, and of keeping one's attention fixed on God.

Ban   A word of hungarian origin. In these texts it designates the second official in charge of a district.

Dikej   From the greek *dikaios*, meaning substitute, vicar.

Dispassion   Freedom from passions, in the sense of no longer yielding to them, although their attacks continue and may be felt. This gift of God brings detachment and peace to the soul; it has nothing in common with indifference or lack of feeling.

Elder   In Slavic, *starec'*; the term means an experienced
            monk, without regard to age, like the honorary
title *abba* of the ancient monks. In the Manjava texts it does not have the specific meaning that it gained only in nineteenth-century Russia, a monk who is a noted spiritual director.

Fear   The term *strax* contains also the meanings of the
          english words 'awe, dread'. The shade of meaning
in each instance is very fine, hence I have consistently translated *strax* as *fear*.

Great Russia   See *Rus'*.

Hierodeacon   A monk ordained deacon.

Hieromonk   A monk ordained priest.

Hieroschemonk   A monk-priest who has assumed the
                   megaloschema, see *Schema*.

Hospodar   Title of the princes of Moldavia and Wallachia.

Ihumen   The superior of a monastery, formally installed. I
            have retained the slavic term in its ukrainian form,
from the greek *hegumenos*, to distinguish the word from others used in the text for superior, since the other words employed have a generic meaning, a superior without reference to a possible title, such as ihumen or even a superior at some work, such as in the kitchen.

Kolyba   A mountain cabin used by shepherds and
            woodcutters.

Ktytor   The term derives from the greek *ktitor,* founder, but it refers also to those who renew a monastery or a church or endow it substantially. A ktytor may have certain rights over the institution, such as that of having a voice in the choice of superior or priest, and the institution has an obligation to remember him perpetually in prayer.

Little Russia   See *Rus'.*

Megaloschema   See *Schema*

Menaion   One of twelve Orthodox liturgical books which make up the *menaia* containing the offices for immovable feasts.

Metochion   A monastic property, distant from the monastery to which it belongs, sometimes even in another country; it is administered by monks sent by the monastery.

Microschema   See *Schema*

Octoechos   The Orthodox liturgical book containing offices for each day of the week arranged according to the eight tones that succeed one another throughout the liturgical year.

Orthodox   The term 'Orthodox' (capital O) at the time these texts were written was not used to designate a particular Church or confession. What today is called the Orthodox Church was then called most often by national names: the Greek Church (applied not only to the Greek Church proper, but to all Churches of the constantinopolitan tradition), the Ruthenian (Ukrainian and Belarus) Church, the Muscovite Church, and so on. In Slavic another term was used to designate this confession, *blahočestie* (*blagočestie* in Russian), literally 'piety', in the sense of devotion to the true faith, and the adjective derived from it, *blahočestyvyj* (*blagočestivyj*). In the Manjava texts, since it is not always clear whether the authors, in writing, *blahočestie, blahočestyvyj,* intend 'piety, pious' or 'Orthodox', I have translated them by the first terms except in a few cases where the second meaning is clearly intended. Where I have 'orthodox' (small o) in the translation, this translates *pravoslavnyj*, which means accepting the doctrines of the first seven ecumenical councils; at that time it likewise was not the name in the Slavic languages for the Orthodox Church, as it is today.

Podvyh   A literal translation would be 'feat', but the english word has unfortunate connotations of exhibitionism, absent in the slavic term. In monastic texts the word refers to ascetic endeavors, but also to all active striving for virtue, even purely interior virtue. *Podvyh* always implies struggle, the overcoming of difficulties, in short, the spiritual combat, be it in fasting or in uprooting anger from one's soul.

Podvyžnyk   A person, most often a monk, who lives a life of *podvyh*.

Polyeleos   Verses from Ps 134 and 135, which repeatedly proclaim God's mercy (*eleos*). They are sung at Matins on most Sundays and on feasts of the greater saints.

Poslušanie   Literally, obedience, and often so translated. This word, however, sometimes refers also to the tasks imposed on a monk, his service, undertaken in obedience, such as the *poslušanie* of baking bread, or even the *poslušanie* of being chosen superior.

Poslušnyk   Literally, obedient. This term is used to designate novices in a monastery.

Rjasa   The outer garment in the habit of a monk or a nun, a long coat, in Ukraine open down the middle, with wide sleeves.

Rus'   The medieval name of the state with Kiev as capital was called *Rus'*. In the seventeenth century Ukrainians used that term, or one derived from it, *Rosija*, to designate their land. *Rus'* and *Rosija*, thus, mean *Ukraine*. Sometimes, however, *Rus'* or *Rosija* refers more specifically to that part of western Ukraine that in civil administration in those times was known as the Rus', or Ruthenian, voevodship, with its center in Lviv. The Russia of today was referred to by its official name at that time, *Muscovy*. Occasionally, terms deriving from greek usage were used: *Little Russia* for Ukraine, *Great Russia* for Russia (Muscovy). In my translation I retain the terms Little Russia, Great Russia, and Muscovy, but translate *Rosija* as *Rus'*.

Ry'zky   A popular name for a kind of edible muchroom found in the Carpathians.

Schema   In Slavic *sxyma*, literally, habit, is used to refer to monastic tonsure, that is, to monastic profession. There are two schemas, *microschema*, the little habit, the profession of all monastics, and *megaloschema*, the great habit, assumed by experienced monastics who aspire to a life of greater austerity. In ukrainian usage, as generally in slavic, the term *sxyma* always refers to the megaloschema.

Sobriety   This is one of the key terms of hesychast spirituality. It signifies a habitual attitude of recollection, with a care not to be carried away by emotions, passions from the remembrance of God.

Solitude   In the texts, *pustynja*, literally desert, a deserted place, wilderness. In the Manjava texts it always refers to a location distant from human settlements.

Starosta   A royal functionary, whose duties ranged over
          fiscal, police, and judicial matters.

Stauropegion   Literally, the setting up of a cross, as a sign of
          a patriarch's direct authority. In the eastern
tradition, a church institution such as a monastery or a
church, which normally would be under the authority of
the local bishop, may be directly under the jurisdiction of
the patriarch; in that case a patriarchal cross is raised there
as a sign of this dependence.

Sticheron   A hymn stanza sung at Matins or Vespers in the
          Orthodox Office.

Stillness   *Bezmolvie* in Slavic is the term used to translate
          the greek *hesychia*, which is here rendered as
stillness. For more on this important concept in eastern
spirituality, see the Introduction.

Strax   See *Fear*

Župnyk   In Moldavia, a title for nobles; in this region of
          the Carpathians it was used either with the same
meaning or to designate a civil official.

Bibliography

TEXTS

The Ante-Nicene Fathers. Vol. 8. Grand Rapids: Eerdmans Publishing Company, 1978.

DESERT FATHERS

Life of Antony by Saint Athanasius of Alexandria. A Select Library of Nicene and Post-Nicene Fathers of the Christian Church. Second Series. Volume 4. Rpt. Grand Rapids: Eerdmans Publishing Company, 1979.

Nikolaas van Wijk. *The Old Church Slavonic Translation of the* Ἀνρῶν Ὁγίων βίβλος *The Hague: Mouton, 1975.*

Dorotheos of Gaza. Discourses and Sayings. Translated Eric P. Wheeler. CS 33. Kalamazoo: Cistercian Publications, 1977.

The Lives of the Desert Fathers. The Historia Monachorum in Aegypto. Translated Norman Russell. CS 34. Kalamazoo: Cistercian Publications, 1981.

Palladius. *The Lausiac History of Palladius.* Translated Cuthbert Butler. Cambridge, 1904.

The Sayings of the Desert Fathers. Translated Benedicta Ward slg. Kalamazoo: Cistercian Publications, 1975.

Les sentences des pères du désert. Translated J. Dion and G. Oury. Abbaye S. Pierre de Solesmes, 1966.

Les sentences des pères du désert. Série des anonymes. Translated Lucien Regnault. Abbaye S. Pierre de Solesmes, 1985.

Helen Waddell. *The Desert Fathers.* London 1936, and reprinted many times.

BASILIAN MONASTICISM

The Ascetic Works of Saint Basil. Translated W.K.L. Clarke. London: Society for Promoting Christian Knowledge, 1925.

Saint Basil. *Ascetical Works.* Translated Monica Wagner. The Fathers of the Church. A New Translation 9. Washington D.C.: The Catholic University of America Press, 1950.

Dans la tradition basilienne. Spiritualité orientale 58. Abbaye de Bellefontaine, 1994.

Lisa Cremaschi. *Nella tradizione basiliana: Costituzioni acetiche, Ammonizione a un figlio spirituale.* Comunità di Bose: Qiqajon, 1997.

Cassian. *Conferences.* Nicene and Post-Nicene Fathers of the Church. Series 2. Volume 11. Rpt. Grand Rapids: Eerdmans Publishing Company, 1978.

Also: *John Cassian. The Conferences.* Translated Boniface Ramsey OP. Ancient Christian Writers, 57. New York: Paulist Press, 1997.

John Climacus. *The Ladder of Divine Ascent.* Translated Colm Luibhead and Norman Russell. The Classics of Western Spirituality. New York: Paulist Press, 1982.

Cyril of Scythopolis. *Lives of the Monks of Palestine.* Translated R. M. Price. CS 114. Kalamazoo: Cistercian Publications, 1991.

Evagrios Pontikos. *Briefe aus der Wüste.* Translated Gabriel Bunge. *Sophia* 24. Trier: Paulinus-Verlag 1986.

Evagrius Ponticus. *The Praktikos and Chapters on Prayer.* Translated John Eudes Bamberger OCSO. CS 4. Spencer 1970.

Isaac le Syrien *Œuvres spirituelles.* Paris 1981.

Symeon the New Theologian. *The Discourses.* Translated C. J. deCatanzaro. The Classics of Western Spirituality. New York: Paulist Press, 1980.

RUSSIAN MONASTICISM

Early Fathers from the Philokalia. Translated E. Kadloubovsky and G. E. H. Palmer. London, 1954.

The Philokalia. Translated and edited G. E. H. Palmer, Philip Sherrard, Kallistos Ware. Vol.1B 4. Faber and Faber. London: Faber and Faber, 1979 , 1990, 1995, 1998.

Writings from the Philokalia on Prayer of the Heart. Translated E. Kadloubovsky and G. E. H. Palmer. London, 1951.

G. P. Fedotov, editor. *A Treasury of Russian Spirituality.* New York 1948.

The Monastic Rule of Iosif Volotsky. Edited and translated David M. Goldfrank. CS 36. Kalamazoo: Cistercian Publications, 1983. Revised edition 2000.

THE BEGINNINGS OF MONASTICISM IN RUS':

The Hagiography of Kievan Rus': Translated Paul Hollingsworth. Harvard Library of Early Ukrainian Literature. English Translations 2. Cambridge, MA: Ukrainian Research Institute of Harvard University, 1992.

The Paterik of the Kievan Caves Monastery. Translated Muriel Heppell. Harvard Library of Early Ukrainian Literature. English Translations 1. Cambridge, MA: Ukrainian Research Institute of Harvard University, 1989.

Sophia Senyk. *A History of the Church in Ukraine.* Volume I: To the End of the Thirteenth Century. Orientalia Christiana Analecta 243. Rome: Pontificio Istituto Orientale, 1993.

Києво-Печерський Патерик. [Kyjevo-Pečrs'kyj Pateryk. Ed. Dmytro Abramovyč]. Kiev 1931; reprint Kiev 1991.

The chronicle quoted from *Полное собрание русских летописей [Polnoe sobranye russkix letopisej],* vol. 1, has been translated into English as *The Russian Primary Chronicle.* Translated and edited by Samuel Hazzard Cross and Olgerd

P. Sherbowitz-Wetzor. Cambridge, Mass.: The Mediaeval Academy of America, 1973.

Hesychast spirituality, and its relation to Palamism:

Pierre Adnés, 'Hésychasme'. *Dictionnaire de spiritualité, 7/1*. Paris 1968. Columns 381–399.

Irénée Hausherr. *La méthode d'oraison hésychaste*. Orientalia Christiana, 36=IX.2. Rome: Pontificio Istituto Orientale, 1927.

Irénée Hausherr. *The Name of Jesus*. Translated Charles Cummings ocso. CS 44. Kalamazoo: Cistercian Publications, 1978.

Irénée Hausherr. *Spiritual Direction in the Early Christian East*. Translated Anthony P. Gythiel. CS 116. Kalamazoo: Cistercian Publications, 1990.

John Meyendorff. *A Study of Gregory Palamas*. Translated George Lawrence. Crestwood: Saint Vladimir Seminary Press, 1974.

John Meyendorff. 'Is "Hesychasm" the Right Word? Remarks on Religious Ideology in the Fourteenth Century', *Harvard Ukrainian Studies*, 7 (1983) 447–456.

The hesychast current in Ukraine:

Elia Citterio. 'La scuola filocalica di Paisij Velichkovskij e la *Filocalia* di Nicodimo Aghiorita. Un confronto'. *Amore del bello. Studi sulla Filocalia*. Comunità di Bose: Qiqajon. 1991.

Ігор Єрьомін, ' "Сводный" Патерик у південно-слов'янських, українському та московському письменствах'. *Записки Історично-Філологічного відділу Української Академії Наук*. [Ihor Jer'omin, 'Svodnyj' Pateryk u pivdenno-slov'jans'kyx, ukrajins'komu ta moskovs'komu pys'menstvax', *Zapysky Istoryčno-Filolohičnoho viddilu Ukrajins'koji Akademiji Nauk,*] 12 (1927).

The Life of Paisij Velyckovs'kyj. Translated J. M. E. Featherstone. Harvard Library of Early Ukrainian Literature. English Translations 4. Cambridge MA: Ukrainian Research Institute of Harvard University, 1989.

Амвросий [Лот оцкий]. *Сказание о Почаевской Успен-ской лавре*. [Amvrosij (Lotockij), *Skazanie o Počaevskoj Uspenskoj lavre*]. Počajiv 1878.

Sophia Senyk, 'L'hésychasme dans le monachisme ukrainien', *Irénikon*, 1989: 172–212.

Sᴏᴜʀᴄᴇꜱ ᴏɴ Mᴀɴᴊᴀᴠᴀ ᴀɴᴅ ʀᴇʟᴀᴛᴇᴅ ǫᴜᴇꜱᴛɪᴏɴꜱ:

Архив юго-западной России. [Arxiv jugo-zapadnoj Rossii]. Part I. 12 volumes. Kiev, 1859–1914.

Юліян Целевич. *Исторія Скиту Манявского*. [Julijan Celevyč. *Istorija Skytu Manjavskoho*]. Lviv 1887.

D. Dorozynskyj. 'Ex actis processus canonizationis gloriosi martyris Josaphat Kuncevicii, Archiep. Polocensis'. In [Josif Slipyj, ed., *Sv. svščm. Josafat Kuncevyč*]. Lviv 1925. Pp.111–232.

С. Голубев. *Киевский митрополит Петр Могила и его сподвижники*. [S. Golubev. *Kievskij mitropolit Petr Mogila i ego spodvižniki*]. Volume 1. Kiev 1883.

Н. Никольский. "Материалы для истории древне-русской духовной письменности". *Известия Отделешия русского языка и словесности* [N. Nikol'skij, 'Materialy dlja istorii drevne-russkoj duxovnoj pis'mennosti', *Izvestija Otdelenija russkogo jazyka i slovesnosti*], 8 (1903), no. 2:65–68.

Памятники, изданные Временною коммисиею для раз-бора древних актов, [Pamjatniki, izdannye Vremennoju kommissieju dlja razbora drevnix aktov]. Vol. 4. Kiev 1859.

S. Josaphat Hieromartyr. Ed. Athanasius G. Welykyj. Volumes 1–2. Rome 1952–1955.

Й. Скрут ень. *'Синопсис* пліснесько-підгорецького монаст иря' [J. Skruten', *'Sinopsis* plisnes'ko-pidhorec'koho monastyrja'], *Analecta Ordinis S. Basilii Magni*, 1/1 (1924) 92–103; 1/2–3 (1925) 306–313; 1/4 (1927) 580–591; 3/1 (1928) 156–164.

Jacobus Susza. *Cursus vitae et certamen martyrii B. Josaphat Kuncevicii.* Paris 1865.

TEXTS CLOSE TO THE SPIRITUAL TRADITION OF MANJAVA.

The Prologue from Ochrid. Lives of the Saints and Homilies for Every Day in the Year. Comp. Nikolai Velimirovic;, Translated Mother Maria. Birmingham, 1985.

Chariton, Igumen of Valamo. *The Art of Prayer. An Orthodox Anthology.* Translated E. Kadloubovsky and G.E.M. Palmer. London: Faber and Faber, 1966.

Hierotheos Vlachos. *A Night in the Desert of the Holy Mountain. Discussion with a Hermit on the Jesus Prayer.* Levadia: Birth of the Theotokos Monastery, 1995².

STUDIES

Sophia Senyk. 'The Eucharistic Liturgy in Ruthenian Church Practice', *Orientalia Christiana Periodica*, 51 (1985) 123–155.

Robert Taft, *The Liturgy of the Hours in East and West.* Collegeville: The Liturgical Press, 1986.

CISTERCIAN PUBLICATIONS

Cistercian Publications publishes in the following areas:

Monastic Texts in English Translation

- The writings of twelfth and thirteenth century Cistercians
- The works of monastic writers in both the eastern and western Church.

Monastic Life, History, Spirituality, Architecture, and Liturgy

- By monks and nuns
- By scholars
- For those with a personal interest in monastic prayer and lifestyle
- For students exploring and
- For scholars specializing in some aspect of the monastic tradition
- Cistercian music and retreat addresses on compact disc and cassette.

To discover other titles in our series of texts and studies in the monastic tradition, please request our free complete catalogue from Customer Service or visit our website:

www.spencerabbey.org/cistpub

Editorial Offices & Customer Service

- Cistercian Publications
  WMU Station, 1903 West Michigan Avenue
  Kalamazoo, Michigan 49008-5415 USA

  Telephone 616 387 8920
  Fax 616 387 8390
  e-mail cistpub@wmich.edu

Canada

- Novalis
  49 Front Street East, Second Floor
  Toronto, Ontario M5E 1B3 CANADA

  Telephone 1 800 204 4140
  Fax 416 363 9409

U.K.

- Cistercian Publications UK
  Mount Saint Bernard Abbey
  Coalville, Leicestershire LE67 5UL UK

- UK Customer Service & Book Orders
  Cistercian Publications
  97 Loughborough Road
  Thringstone, Coalville
  Leicestershire LE67 8LQ UK

  Telephone 01530 45 27 24
  Fax 01530 45 02 10
  e-mail MsbcistP@aol.com

Website & Warehouse

- www.spencerabbey.org/cistpub

- Book Returns (prior permission)
  Cistercian Publications
  Saint Joseph's Abbey
  167 North Spencer Road
  Spencer, Massachusetts 01562-1233 USA

  Telephone 508 885 8730
  Fax 508 885 4687
  e-mail cistpub@spencerabbey.org

Trade Accounts & Credit Applications

- Cistercian Publications / Accounting
  6219 West Kistler Road
  Ludington, Michigan 49431 USA

  Fax 231 843 8919

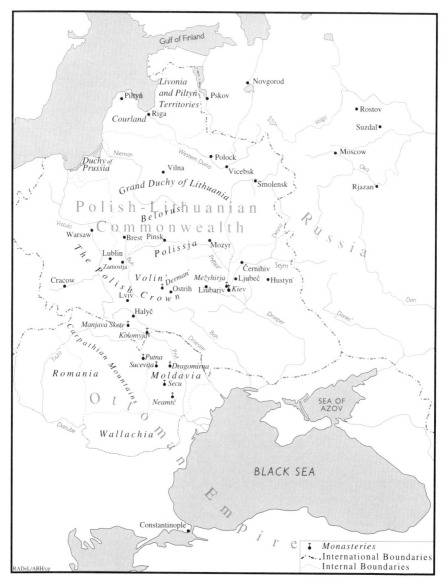

Eastern Europe in the Early Seventeenth Century.